# Giving Voice to Values

# More Praise for *Giving Voice to Values*

"Mary Gentile has responded to the cries of business and business school critics by shifting our attention from debating right versus wrong and right versus right to acting on the questions these dilemmas raise. This is the most significant contribution to business ethics I have experienced in my professional career. It is destined to shape the behavior of future generations in ways that should make us all much prouder of business as an entity and management as a career."

—**Leonard A. Schlesinger,** president, Babson College

"I can think of no better way to take 'ethics' out of the realm of pure philosophical discussion. *Giving Voice to Values* identifies what's stopping us from acting on the values we feel strongly about. It gives us the tools, the courage, and the understanding to be our better selves in even the stickiest business situation."

—**Ira Millstein,** senior partner, Weil, Gotshal, & Manges; senior associate dean for corporate governance and the Eugene F. Williams Jr. Visiting Professor for Competitive Enterprise and Strategy, Yale School of Management

"China as a nation, Chinese corporations, and individual Chinese leaders are all facing a midlife crisis. They are soul searching to decide which way to go for the next stage. They are adults, and adults learn best from their own experience and the experiences of their peers. Nobody can dictate or preach to a successful entrepreneur; their best teacher is their heart, full of wisdom from streetfight experience. All they need is to crystallize their internal values through a process of external expression. *Giving Voice to Values* is doing just that and that is exactly what China needs. Launching GVV in China will be a striking success, and it will be critical to China's continued success."

—**Dr. Morley C. Su,** president of Millennium Capital Services, a leading climate change solutions provider in China

MARY C. GENTILE

# Giving Voice to Values

## How to Speak Your Mind When You Know What's Right

Yale
UNIVERSITY
PRESS
New Haven and London

Published with assistance from the Louis Stern Memorial Fund.

The Preface is reprinted, with revision, from the February 5, 2009, issue of *BusinessWeek* by special permission, copyright ©2010 by The McGraw-Hill Companies, Inc.

Designed by Sonia Shannon
Set in Minion by Integrated Publishing Solutions
Printed in the United States of America by Sheridan Books,
Ann Arbor, Michigan.

*The Library of Congress has cataloged the hardcover edition as follows:*
Gentile, Mary C.
Giving voice to values : how to speak your mind when
you know what's right / Mary C. Gentile.
p. cm.
Includes bibliographical references and index.
ISBN 978-0-300-16118-2 (alk. paper)
1. Business ethics. 2. Leadership. 3. Values. I. Title.
HF5387.G464 2010
174—dc22 2010011905

ISBN 978-0-300-18156-2 (pbk.)

A catalogue record for this book is available from the British Library.

10 9 8 7 6 5

*To all those who would like to voice their values…*
*rather than wonder whether they can*

# Contents

# Preface

Whether you were among those who lauded the clarity of President Barack Obama's Inaugural Address in 2009 or those who bemoaned its lack of quotable quotes, you most likely heard his call for an "era of responsibility" loud and clear. In fact, when he turned to the topic of greatest concern for the electorate—the economic downturn— he plainly stated that the nation's woes were the result not only of "greed and irresponsibility on the parts of some" but also, and more important for the path out of this mess, of "the collective failure to make hard choices" by the rest of us.

The credit market meltdown and governance misbehavior had, once again, triggered conversations among business leaders, business educators, and the business press about just what they were communicating and teaching in the halls of industry, in corporate training seminars, and in business schools. After all, you didn't have to look far to find a lot of highly trained and highly placed managers doing a perp walk. Even more disconcerting were all those business school graduates who may not have crossed the legal line but who had presided over, or at least given silent assent to, a stream of decisions that led to the collapsing dominoes of the worldwide financial system.

What we cannot afford, however, is for businesses and business education to respond to this internal and external critique in the same way we have responded to scandals in the past. It is no longer acceptable to merely bemoan the problem of a "few bad apples" and then focus on preparing future business leaders to develop *awareness* of the kinds of ethical breaches they might encounter in their careers—presumably so they can recognize them in time to choose not to work for those bad actors and thereby avoid the problem.

The other most common approach is to focus on the difficulty of reasoning our way through knotty and challenging ethical dilemmas where the answers are not black and white but many shades of gray. The focus is on those big, thorny issues where reasonable and intelligent people of goodwill may quite understandably disagree, and often do. These case studies can trigger what one Harvard professor called "ethics fatigue." The training and educational focus is on *analysis* and the ethical reasoning models that philosophers have probed for centuries: duty-based decision making, rights-based decision making, utilitarian decision making, and so on.

Unfortunately, whether future managers find such discussions intellectually engaging or tedious and irrelevant, too often all they learn is how to frame an argument to justify virtually any position no matter how cynical or self-serving. Utilitarianism, after all, is tailor-made for a free-market economy. I remember one CEO who told me that while interviewing a recent MBA graduate for a job, he asked the man whether he had taken a course in business ethics. When the interviewee answered yes, the CEO asked him what he had learned. The job candidate explained that he had learned about all the models of ethical analysis—deontology, virtue ethics, consequentialism, and so on—and that whenever he encountered a conflict, he could decide what he wanted to do and then select the model of ethical reasoning that would best support his choice. Needless to say, this was probably not the intended lesson of the class.

The first approach described above is about *awareness* and *avoidance*. The second is about *analysis*. But what we really need now is preparation and practice for *action*, and not just any action but a particular kind of hard, often risky, intricate values-based action.

The typical business ethics discussion or classroom is too often a kind of school for scandal, where managers review case studies and then spend all their time outlining the many reasons why being ethical is not so easy, or even so clear after all. Often we hear: "Well, when I'm CEO I can take action on this kind of decision, but as a middle manager, I have neither the power nor the influence to do so." On the other hand, when managers put themselves in the place of the CEO, they say: "Well, if I were lower in the organization, I might be able to take this kind of personal risk and stand up against this behavior. But I have the jobs and lives of thousands of employees and investors depending on me. I can't afford the luxury of having values." Sounds like Chuck Prince in July 2007, not long before he was deposed as the head of Citigroup, when he said: "As long as the music is playing, you've got to get up and dance."

It's not that ethical theory and high-level strategic dilemmas are not important; they are. But they don't help future managers and leaders figure out what to do next—when a boss wants to alter the financial report, or their sales team applies pressure to misrepresent the capabilities of their product, or they witness discrimination against a peer—and these are the experiences that will shape their ability to take on the big, strategic, thorny ethical dilemmas in due time.

The near-term skills needed to deal with these kinds of challenges concern knowing what to say, to whom, and how to say it when a manager knows what he or she thinks is right in a particular situation—but doesn't feel confident about how to *act* on his or her convictions. This overlooked but consequential skill is the first step in building the ethical muscle.

This is the purpose of Giving Voice to Values, an innovative approach to the development of practical, principled leadership in business. Although developed for use in the business classroom, with the Aspen Institute Business and Society Program as incubator and founding partner along with the Yale School of Management as the second founding partner, and now with ongoing support from Babson College, the approach is spreading beyond the business classroom to other disciplines and to corporate training settings. Through this book and other recent materials, it offers a framework and set of insights and tools that will also equip individual readers with the skills, the scripts, and the confidence to act on their most deeply held values in the workplace.

The main idea behind Giving Voice to Values (GVV) is the observation that a focus on *awareness* of ethical issues and on *analysis* of what the right thing to do may be is insufficient. Precious little time is spent on *action*—that is, developing the "scripts" and implementation plans for responding to the commonly heard "reasons and rationalizations" for questionable practices, and actually practicing the delivery of those scripts.

GVV is all about this neglected area of scripts and action plans and practice: building the skills, the confidence, the moral muscle, and, frankly, the *habit* of voicing our values. It begins with the assumption that most of us want to bring our whole selves to work—skills, ambitions, and values. Yet we know from experience and research that most of us will encounter values conflicts in our careers, when the way we want to live and the things we want to accomplish seem in conflict with the expectations of our clients, our peers, our bosses, or our organizations. That is why this skill and practice-based approach is essential.

In its own way, Giving Voice to Values is a resounding response to President Obama's inaugural call for the rest of us to be more willing and able to make the hard

choices. Without denying the value of building awareness and developing stronger analytical skills, GVV is
premised on the assumption that in many if not most of
the managerial and financial misbehaviors that we have
seen in the past, there were enough people who recognized the lapses in ethics and judgment to have stopped
them. The problem was that they did not believe it was
possible to do so.

The conviction behind GVV—one that is supported
by both qualitative research as well as cognitive neuro-
science studies—is that, simply stated, practice makes
perfect, or at least, practice makes our voice and action
more likely. After all, despite unprecedented complexity
in financial products like credit default swaps, the reasons we give for why we do what we do are pretty familiar: *I didn't think we'd get caught... ; I didn't know how to
say no... ; Everyone else was doing it... ;* and so on. If we
get comfortable responding to *those* arguments, in fresh,
persuasive, nondefensive ways, just think what might
happen.

Perhaps most important, if we—business students
and individual managers and business leaders—have the
opportunity to work together to craft our "scripts" for
responding to these rationalizations, we can also begin to
see these statements not as coming from a place of self-
righteousness—something few of us can truly claim and
a stance that rarely wins followers—but as coming from
a place of competence and conviction. Or, as the president might say, from a place of collective responsibility.

## About This Book

Based on interviews and current research in management and social psychology, this book weaves together illustrative stories—notably often positive exemplars—with specific guidelines and a tested methodology for preparing ourselves to plan, script, and execute effective strategies for implementing our values in times of ethical conflict. Unlike most books about business ethics, the focus of GVV is post–decision making (a phrase coined by Carolyn Woo, the dean of Notre Dame University's business school to describe the approach). It is not about deciding what the right thing to do is, but rather about how to get it done.

Because the focus of GVV is different from the usual discussion of business ethics, therefore the focus and style of this book will be different from the usual business ethics text. In fact, in many ways this is a book more about action than about ethics; about stories, both sharing them and creating them, than about analysis; and about learning to be more of who we already are, rather than about learning to become better or other than that.

The book works well in an educational context because it includes case examples for discussion; a set of concepts illustrated with stories and supported with a bibliography of relevant research; and a straightforward and simple methodology for building and testing effective "values scripts." In fact, curricular materials, including case studies, exercises, readings, self-assessment tools, and teaching plans, are available online for use with this approach (www.GivingVoiceToValues.org). I developed many of these materials in collaboration with business practitioners who have shared their stories; increasingly, other faculty and graduate business students from different parts of the world have been inspired to contribute to the ever expanding collection. These stories and discussions about them are engaging and instructive for the individual reader as well, especially because the book is written in a conversational style. Although based on much relevant scholarly research on the questions of business ethics, values, and voice, this book is more of a primer on how we can enact these commitments than a report on the scholarship.

Another distinguishing feature of Giving Voice to Values is its origin. This book has grown not only out of research and interviews (nothing new there), but also from the development, successful global launch, and ongoing expansion of an innovative business education curriculum. The GVV curriculum has been adopted for MBA, executive, and undergraduate business education in more than a hundred pilots, in locations as diverse as the United States, China, India, South Africa, Australia, Canada, Europe, and the Middle East.

Finally, as we shall see in this book, one of the enablers of effective values-based action is the explicit and broad definition of our purpose. In that spirit, the bold but sincere purpose of Giving Voice to Values is not just to transform the foundational assumptions of the teaching of practical, principled management, but also to equip future business leaders to know what is right *and* how to make it happen.

# Acknowledgments

Many organizations and individuals have helped make this book possible and, more important, contributed their insights and support to the development of the Giving Voice to Values concept and initiative.

Thank you to GVV's founding partners, the Aspen Institute Business and Society Program and Yale School of Management, for their early faith in this initiative and their financial support. In particular, my gratitude to Judith Samuelson for her vision and confidence, Joel Podolny for his willingness to make a leap of faith, and the Robert J. Silver '50 Fund for Innovation in Management Education at the Yale School of Management for its investment. At the Aspen Institute, thank you also to Chad Ayotte, Rebecca Darr, Justin Goldbach, John Hollwitz, Suzanne Lanza, Rich Leimsider, Linda Lehrer, Nancy McGaw, Neela Pal, Sarah Reinhoff, Sangeeta Renade, Alex Roberts, Rachel Shattuck, and the rest of the staff who have supported this work. At Yale School of Management, a special thank you to Ira Millstein, who worked with me to develop materials and who, along with Daylian Cain, piloted this work in their courses.

Thank you to the Fetzer Institute and Thomas Beech for their support of the early pilot study, and to Columbia Graduate School of Business for important and formative lessons learned from its commitment to raise and explore ethics and values-driven leadership in the curriculum. In particular at Columbia, thank you to Ray Horton, Paul Glasserman, Sandra Navalli, Mike Feiner, Bruce Kogut, William Klepper, Sharon Sarosky, Clelia Peters, Joel Brockner, and Daniel Ames.

I am grateful to Babson College, in particular Len Schlessinger and Shahid Ansari, for their more recent engagement and deep commitment to this work, both financially as well as intellectually, and their dedication to extending its impact on global curricula in entrepreneurial thought and action.

Much gratitude goes to all the business practitioners who generously shared their time and experiences and learning gained from voicing their values as the basis of the insights and case examples here. Thanks also to the many faculty members and institutions that have been early intellectual contributors, adopters, and supporters, as well as partners in the development of materials and teaching. They are too numerous to name, but a number of individuals require particular thanks: Minette Drumwright at the University of Texas, Austin; Carolyn Woo and Jessica McManus at Notre Dame Mendoza College of Business; Ranjini Swamy at Goa Institute of Management; Leigh Hafrey and Neil Hartman at the Massachusetts Institute of Technology; J. D. Schramm and Beth Benjamin at Stanford University; Jane Cote, Joseph Cote, Jerry Goodstein, and Claire Latham at Washington State University, Vancouver; Maureen Scully at the University of Massachusetts, Boston; Cynthia Ingols, Deborah Marlino, Sylvia Maxfield, Deborah Merrill-Sands, Paul Myers, and Mary Shapiro at Simmons School of Management; Linda Hill, Joseph Badaracco, Thomas Piper, Michael Jensen, Sandra Sucher, and Bill Ellet at Harvard Business School; Henri-Claude de Bettignies at Euro-China Centre for Leadership and Responsibility of the China-Europe International Business School (CEIBS) in Shanghai; N. Craig Smith, INSEAD; Zucheng Zhou at Antai College of Economics and Management, Shanghai Jiao Tong University; Morley Su, president of Energy Systems International and director of corporate strategy for the Pacific Millennium Group; Linda Angell and Andy Klein at the American University of Sharjah, United Arab Emirates; David Webb, Mark Edwards, and Stacie Chappell at the University of Western Australia Business School, Perth; Ram Ramnarayan at the Indian School of Business, Hyderabad; Piya Mukherjee, Mumbai; Marcy Crary, Tony Buono, and Rosa Lee Hunter at Bentley College; Jean Kilgore and Robin Dubin at Case Western Reserve University; Mark Dillard at Emory University; Mark Mallinger at Pepperdine University; Christopher Adkins at the College of William and Mary; Roy Lewicki at Ohio State University; Michael Santoro at Rutgers University; Robin Johnson at the University of California, Los Angeles; Daniel Arce, University of Texas, Dallas; George Brenkert at Georgetown University; Dolores Heffernan Smith at University College, Dublin; Margie Parikh at Gujarat University; Jody Hoffer Gittell at Brandeis University; Cliff Hakim; Jorge Fontanez; Gina Vega at

Salem State College; Daniel Malan and Jako Volschenk at University of Stellenbosch Business School, South Africa.

Thank you most especially to my editor at Yale University Press, Michael O'Malley, who saw the book even before I did and has been unfailingly supportive throughout its development.

Most important and always, thank you to my life's partner, my best friend, my intellectual and emotional touchstone and wish-fulfilling jewel, Mary H. Jacobsen.

# Introduction

This book begins with the assumption that most of us want to find ways to voice and act on our values in the workplace, and to do so effectively. The focus here is on those times and situations when we believe we know what is right and want to do it, but we experience external pressures—from our boss, our colleagues, our customers—to do otherwise. As a result, we are not sure how to raise our concerns. The focus here is not so much on situations where we are tempted to do something we believe is wrong, for our own personal gain or because we think we can get away with it. While that is a relevant topic, it is one for another day.

Most outcries about unethical behavior in business tend to focus on personal greed or ambition, but this book is concerned with those times when we are really not grabbing for money or power. The thesis here is that if enough of us felt empowered—and were skillful and practiced enough—to voice and act on our values effectively on those occasions when our best selves are in the driver's seat, business would be a different place. In other words, this book is not about changing who we are, but rather it is about empowering the parts of us that already want to do the right thing. Even though we may all sometimes act unethically, the fact is that we all do sometimes also act ethically. This book is about expanding that second set.

Some might say that what we really want is to be able to *feel* like we have voiced and acted on our values. And this desire may lead us just as easily—perhaps more easily—to focus our energy on finding ways to rationalize what we say and do such that it appears consistent with our values, as opposed to focusing our energy on finding ways to actually be consistent with our values. Research on self-bias offers some support for this view.[1]

Others might point out that the real challenge before us is one of efficacy. That is, given the organizational and personal barriers to acting on our values, success in this arena can be mighty elusive. Thus even if we don't succumb to the self-justifying bias noted above, many—if not most—of us will abandon attempts to follow our values simply because we don't believe it is possible to do so.[2] We may believe that despite our best efforts and courage, we will not be able to change the offending organizational practice or influence the offending individuals, especially if they are our superiors in the organization or if they appear to be in the majority.

In addition, we may fear the price we would be forced to pay—anything from social disapproval to negative career consequences or financial and family disruptions. Certainly research on whistle-blowers who speak up outside their own organization to the media, the police, or regulatory bodies suggests that they often suffer both personally and professionally. And although the type of action we are talking about here precedes, and hopefully makes unnecessary, external whistle-blowing, there can be negative consequences even for those who raise uncomfortable questions inside their organizations. We all have seen, heard, or at least can imagine stories of individuals who raised unpopular or uncomfortable questions and were subsequently seen as naive or less than committed to doing what it takes to succeed.[3] They may be excluded from the inner circle or from the conversations where real strategy is set, thereby hurting their career trajectory and limiting their ability to have an impact anyway.

And of course it is important not to underestimate how difficult it can be to even know what our own core values are, and whether or not a particular practice conflicts with them. As has been often pointed out by thoughtful people, ranging from ethicists to political scientists, many of the thorniest choices we face in our lives are less about right versus wrong than about right versus right. If this were not the case, a consequentialist approach to ethics (weighing the relative costs and benefits of different actions) would be both easier to apply and much less necessary. As Robert Kane writes in *Through the Moral Maze:* "The first of many confusions that people have about ethics concerns the value of thinking about it. Ethical argument is not primarily directed at those who are bent on doing evil. It is directed in the first instance not at bad people, but at good people whose convictions are being drained by intellectual and moral confusions."[4]

Given all these caveats and concerns about the framing of our opening assumption here—that is, the assumption that most of us want to find ways to voice and act on our values in the workplace, and to do so effectively—it is important to clarify that this book is not about denying the very human tendency to rationalize in the service of self-justification. It does not downplay the obstacles to effective action in the face of values conflicts, or try to deny the risks. It does not even seek to avoid the complexities involved in actually clarifying what actions best support our values.

Rather, this book is about acknowledging that nevertheless, some people *do* voice and act on their values, and do so effectively. There is much to be learned from looking at how and why they do so. They do so not simply in spite of each of the above objections, but also because of their sophisticated understanding of the objections themselves. That is, they make an effort to know themselves and to better understand others, diminishing the impact of self-justifying rationalizations. They think strategically about how to implement their values, thereby diminishing the risks they face; and when the risks are unavoidable, they view them clear-eyed and prepare themselves. After all, risk management is not always about avoiding risks; rather it is often about anticipating, preparing for, and mitigating them. And they learn to communicate about values openly and clearly, thus ensuring that they have access to more and better information with which to make considered decisions. That is, we are talking about efforts to make change within an organization via problem redefinition, creative problem solving, constructive engagement, persuasion, reasoning, personal example, and leadership.

This book is about ways to think about and accomplish all of these things and so finally, this book is about acknowledging and enabling choice.

## The Origins of Giving Voice to Values

In 2006, the Aspen Institute Business and Society Program approached the Yale School of Management with an invitation to become founding partners, with Aspen as incubator, for the launch of the Giving Voice to Values initiative. GVV is a program of research and curriculum development designed to analyze and share the many ways that business practitioners can and do voice and implement their values in the face of countervailing pressures in the workplace. The lessons learned from this program are the subject of this book, but before delving into those lessons, it is useful to understand its origins.

The approach to values born from this initiative and described in this book grows out of a rich set of inputs. As we will see in subsequent pages, the power and effectiveness of our efforts to voice and act on our values are often driven by the power and persuasiveness of the stories we tell about them. Therefore, let us begin with the story of how the approach described here was born— both the personal story and the public story.

First, the personal story.[5] When I started work at a business school—the Harvard Business School in the mid-1980s—I experienced culture shock. This was a time when even the student newspapers at business schools crowed that students would attempt a hostile takeover of their grandmothers if they could make a profit at it.

I was fresh out of graduate school with a doctorate in the humanities and nothing had prepared me for this new world. I was excited by the energy, the clarity of intention, and the sheer logic of the place. It seemed the opposite of everything I had known. I would joke with my friends that when my fellow doctoral students in literature and film used to ask, "How are you?" I would be considered suspect—either shallow or ignorant—if I answered without the requisite level of angst seasoned with knowing despair. At the business school, on the other hand, the accepted response to such a greeting was "Great, just great!" delivered in a firm and confident tone accompanied by direct eye contact, preferably with an energetic pumping of one's right arm and closed fist. What looking glass had I stumbled through?

Business school and the corporate offices of senior executives I frequented as a researcher, case writer, and eventual faculty member were halls of purposefulness and confidence. Whereas the test of intelligence in my life had previously been the ability to take a single passage of poetry or fiction and open it up, revealing multiple layers of meaning and nuance, the performance test here seemed to be the ability to define a problem so precisely and cleanly that all irrelevancy fell away and one was left with a clearly solvable equation or a single principle to optimize. It was a beautiful and heady world, albeit one to which I was unaccustomed.

Twenty-plus years after my introduction to that world, we live in a time when the once astonishing mergers and acquisitions deals of the 1980s are surpassed and even dwarfed on a regular basis. It is a time when CEOs, having risen to the status of popular heroes in the late 1990s, face heightened public scrutiny as a result of the widely publicized and stunning excesses and abuses of the early 2000s, followed by a devastating financial crisis from which we have not yet recovered. But despite this fall from grace, belief in the power and efficacy of business has not diminished; rather, it is the public's trust in the business agenda and its methods that has been tarnished. In fact, the degree of public and government scrutiny and even cynicism that business and its leaders encounter today is a direct reflection of the amount of power, control, and capacity they are believed to wield.

This brings us to a fundamental irony about leadership in this arena. Business leaders and aspiring business leaders in free-market contexts are attracted to the potential to make an impact, to build something tangible, to manage and control an enterprise, and, of course, to make money. This is a world of "can do" attitudes, of belief in the individual's capacity to make a difference by sheer dint of talent and hard work. Yet when it comes to social impacts and ethical action, these business practitioners all too often protest that their hands are tied. When it comes to running their business in a manner that explicitly serves society, through both the values it creates and also the values it preserves, they often appear to believe that the market prevents them from doing as much as they might wish. I find myself wondering how the arena of free-market capitalism, so steeped in the orthodoxy of individualism and a belief in the mastery of one's own fate, can be so constrained. Is there free will in business?

The Giving Voice to Values initiative is a response to this irony.

Moving from the personal story, let us consider some of the other inputs to this work. In 2001 and 2002, the Aspen Institute conducted a survey of MBA student attitudes regarding the role of business in society. When asked whether they expected they would have to make business decisions that conflicted with their personal values during their careers, half the respondents in 2002 (and more than half in 2001) believed that they would. The vast majority of respondents both years reported it would be "very likely" or "somewhat likely" that they would experience this as stressful. And in 2001, over half of respondents said their response to such a conflict would be to look for another job; in 2002 that number declined to 35 percent, still a significant number. One in five students reported that their business education was not preparing them at all to manage such conflicts, and the majority said they were being prepared only "somewhat."[6]

Student and faculty reports from business schools reinforce this observation that students expect to encounter values conflicts during their careers. In fact, they have already faced them by the time they return to graduate school. A few years ago as part of a concerted effort to address values and ethics issues in the curriculum, Columbia Business School invited incoming MBA students to write a one-page essay about a time when they had experienced a conflict between their values and what they were asked to do in the workplace.

The conflicts these young managers described in hundreds of essays were often quite similar—pressure to overstate or understate billable hours; to adjust economic forecasts; to adjust earnings reports; to inflate product capabilities or understate the time needed to provide services; to place organizational priorities above individual responsibilities and loyalties; and so on.[7]

But despite the similar stories they told, these students' responses were sometimes quite different. Many reported their discomfort with such conflicts but a quiet acceptance of the impossibility of resisting the organizational demands. Others, while reporting seemingly identical conflicts and pressures, decided to voice their objections and found ways—sometimes very creative ways—to resolve the conflicts. These students did not appear to be more articulate or more intelligent. Their essays did not express a greater sense of discomfort than the essays of those who did not voice or act on their values. They did, however, make the decision to say something. Sometimes they spoke persuasively; sometimes they appeared to be a bit naive or clumsy. Some succeeded in changing the practice they addressed; others did not. But they spoke up, and that put them on a different path. The question becomes: What enables the choice to speak up?

The Aspen Institute study and the business school student stories bring to mind some research conducted on "Rescuers" in World War II (individuals who risked their own safety to assist those threatened by the Nazis), in an effort to identify the factors held in common by those who have been known to act with moral courage in the face of danger. One of the key characteristics these subjects tended to share was the experience, earlier in their lives, of anticipating situations where their values would be challenged and sharing out loud with a respected listener what they would do—a kind of pre-scripting.[8]

And thus the "Giving Voice to Values" initiative was born. The approach to values conflicts described here provides managers and students of management with the opportunity to identify with someone who knows what their values dictate in a particular situation—as opposed to someone who is wondering what the right thing to do in a situation might be (as is often the case in traditional corporate conversations and academic ethics workshops)—and then to script their response. In other words, this approach is *post–decision making*. It is not about analyzing what the right thing to do might be or whether to act on our values in the workplace; it's about starting from the assumption that we know what we want to do and then figuring out how we might make that happen—and, very importantly, practicing our voice in front of peers who stand in as proxies for our workplace colleagues.

Of course, many of the thorniest ethical problems in business today are not at all clear-cut. However, in those cases where intelligent people of goodwill may honestly disagree about what the "right" thing to do is, having practiced the skills and scripts necessary to effectively voice values-based positions will make better decisions more likely, because more well-reasoned and well-articulated positions will be in the mix of the workplace conversation. As this book makes clear, the process of GVV involves explicitly identifying the stakes for all parties in any situation and, importantly, developing responses to the reasons and rationalizations used to defend the questioned course of action. Practice and eventual fluency with this process enables folks to become more clear-sighted about the hitherto ambiguous situations.

In fact, many of the times when we think the ethics of an issue is unclear, or even when we don't see the values conflict at all, this ambiguity or invisibility is actually a second-order response. That is, because we have so internalized that it will not be possible to raise a concern or change the situation, we (often unconsciously) begin to craft ways of seeing the situation that obscure the values conflict. This is a kind of preemptive rationalization, if you will. If we felt more confident that voice and action were possible, we would be able to see the issues more clearly, or at least be able to raise the questions that make our collective clarity possible.

However, when all is said and done, even after we have decided what we want to do, acting on that choice is not easy, and the courage and quality of implementation can be as important as, or sometimes even more important than, the quality of the choice. That implementation is at the core of this book.

This is not to say that finding "successful" resolutions to values conflicts is easy, or even always possible. Rather this book simply suggests that people do try; that it is important and worthwhile to try; and that such resolutions are, in fact, sometimes possible. This is an important distinction—the difference between not knowing the answer to the question of how to implement our values and not believing that there could be such an answer. This is often an unspoken struggle within managers, as well as business educators. In fact, one of the reasons why managers and educators are sometimes uncomfortable with explicit discussions of the ethical implications of managerial actions may well be because they are not necessarily convinced that it is, in fact, possible to voice our values successfully. This suggests a need to pay attention to both the approaches that enable us to voice our values successfully as well as our very definition of "success" in these instances.

Accordingly, this book looks at ways to learn from business practitioners who have already acted on their values. Although informed by research, the stories and approach described here are practical. This book does not suggest that the identified strategies always work, or even prove that a particular response is the "right" one. Rather it posits a laboratory where discussants—both current managers and students of business—can pursue a thought experiment and explicitly ask: "What *if* you were going to act on your values—what would you say and do?"

Such a seemingly straightforward question is not often posed in business decision-making meetings or classrooms—save for the final moments of a discussion where the bulk of time was spent identifying countervailing pressures and reasons why we might not pursue our values—and they can have real impact when they are raised. When addressed in depth, these questions take the discussion out of the realm of right and wrong and into the realm of practice—a terrain where discussants, students, and businesspeople alike are often more comfortable, and which triggers that can-do attitude that seems to become peculiarly disabled when a question is framed as one of ethics and social responsibility.

The appeal of this approach is supported by the early and enthusiastic responses to the Giving Voice to Values curriculum. With only limited promotion and word-of-mouth encouragement, GVV is already being piloted in business schools on five continents, and companies have begun to work on ways to adapt the approach for their own internal training purposes.

In the pages that follow, we will discuss some lenses or ways of thinking about values in the workplace that appear to enable managers to ask and answer the question, "What if we were going to act on our values—what would we say and do?" When we view values conflicts through these lenses, our confidence and capacity to voice and act on our values can be greatly enhanced.

## How This Book Is Organized

The book is divided into nine chapters, which walk the reader through the various assumptions behind its practical approach to values conflicts and discuss examples of how these ways of thinking can lead to effective and usable scripts and action plans for voicing our values.[9]

### CHAPTER 1
### GIVING VOICE TO OUR VALUES: THE THOUGHT EXPERIMENT

The opening chapter explains the thought experiment at the heart of the Giving Voice to Values approach and clarifies why this framing is important. For the experiment to have traction, the working hypotheses behind it must be explicit, so this chapter names our twelve starting assumptions and explains the reasoning and the stories behind them. These assumptions describe the attitudes, beliefs, and capacities that enable our efforts to voice and act on our values. The chapter invites readers to suspend disbelief and try on an approach to values-based behavior that can draw the best from us, fueling creativity, confidence, and skillful execution.

As Michael C. Jensen, the Jesse Isidor Straus Professor of Business Administration Emeritus at Harvard Business School, puts it: "GVV shifts the focus away from debates about what the 'right' answer to an ethical challenge might be and places the focus on how to act on one's values in a particular situation. This approach provides people the opportunity to practice handling the discomfort, threats, isolation, and embarrassment people face in such situations."

Finally, the first chapter points out that GVV is an individual strategy and that individuals exist within organizations that can limit or enhance the options available to address values conflicts. This reality is mentioned not as a reason to avoid voicing our values, but as another opportunity to reframe the choice. This book shares stories to illustrate strategies available for us to act as individuals within organizations that may not always be supportive.

The next seven chapters each explore one of the pillars or foundational concepts in the Giving Voice to Values approach.

CHAPTER 2

VALUES: WHAT THEY ARE
AND WHAT THEY ARE NOT

Although we may quibble around the edges, knowing that, in general, certain values are widely shared gives us both a useful (because of its commonality) and manageable (because of its brevity) foundation to which we can refer when trying to address values conflicts in the workplace. Recognizing that our differences or disagreements about values, though real, do not preclude the development and pursuit of shared goals is a useful primary position to adopt when we think about how to voice and act on those values. Chapter 2 identifies the types of values that are widely shared—across cultures and contexts—and also those that may not be. Stories illustrate the different ways to effectively appeal to the most commonly shared values when facing ethical conflicts, as well as the mindset needed to be effective in doing so—avoiding parochialism, preaching, paternalism, and pettiness.

CHAPTER 3

A TALE OF TWO STORIES:
THE POWER OF CHOICE

We have noticed an interesting phenomenon in our interviews with managers and students. When asked to talk about a time when they experienced a values conflict in the workplace and how they handled it, they engage in some interesting self-reflection. The level of self-examination possible when one begins from the premise that someone *has* acted on their values is striking. This starting point seems to free them up to raise the counterexamples—perhaps because they feel less defensive.

Recognizing the fact that we are all capable of speaking and acting on our values, as well as the fact that we have not always done so, is both empowering and enlightening. The managerial stories in Chapter 3 illustrate the freedom, creativity, and confidence that are unleashed once values conflicts are truly embraced as *choices*. Exercises to encourage this kind of self-recognition and tools for this kind of problem reframing are outlined.

## CHAPTER 4
### IT'S ONLY NORMAL

If we approach our business careers with the expectation that we will face values conflicts and if we anticipate some of the most common types of conflicts in our own intended industry and functional area, we can minimize the disabling effect that surprise can have. We will also likely find ourselves framing our attempts to speak about these issues in a less emotional manner and more as a matter of course. Such an approach can have the effect of normalizing and defusing the topic not only for ourselves but also for the individuals with whom we hope to discuss them. Additionally, by anticipating and normalizing the idea that we will have to take risks—even career-threatening ones—at some point in our work lives, we expand our vision of what the degrees of freedom are in our decision making.

Chapter 4 illustrates the powerful impact that this kind of normalization can have through managerial sto-

ries and provides tools for building this kind of frame
and set of expectations in ourselves.

## CHAPTER 5
### WHAT AM I WORKING FOR?

If we define our professional purpose explicitly and
broadly (including means as well as ends, for example, or
addressing impacts beyond short-term profitability), we
have an easier time seeing values conflicts as an expected
part of doing business, with costs and benefits that do
not seem unusual or especially daunting in comparison
with other business challenges.

Chapter 5 discusses the different levels of purpose
(personal, professional, organizational, societal) and illustrates the differential impacts of a narrow versus a
broad purpose definition at each level. Managerial stories illustrate how we can take control of our own purpose, by naming it explicitly and by working out a map
of intersections among and between the different levels.
Seeming conflicts can be reframed as conscious choices
when the issue of purpose is addressed explicitly.

## CHAPTER 6
### PLAYING TO MY STRENGTHS: SELF-
### KNOWLEDGE, SELF-IMAGE, AND ALIGNMENT

Given the strength and energy that come from acting in
a way that is in alignment with our core self, we can en-

hance our willingness and ability to voice and act on our values by finding a way to view ourselves—by writing a "self-story," if you will—that integrates acting on our values with our sense of who we truly are. If we see ourselves as "pragmatists," for example, let us find a way to view voicing our values as pragmatic.

Chapter 6 illustrates how individual managers have reframed their ethical choices to align them with a self-image in which they felt most comfortable and most competent at voicing their values. The chapter presents a set of self-assessment criteria—identified through our interviews with managers who have already successfully acted on their values—and suggestions for crafting a "self-story" that provides clues as to how to reframe the values conflicts each of us may encounter so that voicing our values will be the most comfortable default position.

## CHAPTER 7
### FINDING MY VOICE

To make it more likely that we do speak up about values conflicts in the workplace, it is important to recognize that there are many different ways to express our values (for example, assertion, questioning, research, and providing new data; persuasion, negotiation, setting an example, identifying allies); that some may work better in some circumstances than others; that we may be more skillful or simply more likely to use one approach than another, and so our ability to see a way to use that particular approach may be the most important determining factor in whether or not we speak; that some organizational contexts and conditions (and some sorts of leaders) will have a strong impact on our own and others' likelihood of expressing values; and that there are things we can do to make it more likely that we will voice our values and that we will do so effectively: namely, reflection, practice, and coaching.

Chapter 7 illustrates research findings about the likelihood and impact of self-expression with individual stories of managers who developed a voice over the course of a career. The impacts of organizational culture and relationships on our ability to use our voice are emphasized, as well as ways that individuals may work to reframe and revise these organizational impacts when necessary.

This chapter also revisits the idea of a "self-story," introduced in the previous chapter, and suggests that the way we frame our level and position within our careers and within our own story can either encourage or discourage voice. There are degrees of freedom and different constraints that we experience differently depending on our age, level of experience, seniority in a firm or in a profession, positional power, and so on. Rather than using one's particular position in life, a firm, or a career as a rationale for limiting our options for voice, GVV explicitly reframes these realities—or rewrites the story—so that we can find the power in our positions.

CHAPTER 8

REASONS AND RATIONALIZATIONS

When we encounter values conflicts in the workplace, we often face barriers in the form of "reasons and rational-izations" for pursuing a particular course of action that can confound our best attempts to fulfill our own sense of organizational and personal purpose. One Harvard professor even called these "professional rationalizations."

If we begin to recognize categories of argument or reasons that we typically hear when someone is defend-ing a behavior that feels ethically questionable, we can develop and practice some useful questions, persuasive arguments, and ways of framing our own role or pur-pose, as well as that of our organization, which can help us respond persuasively to these common arguments. Finally, the act of recognizing and naming the category of argu-ment can reduce its power because it is no longer uncon-scious or assumed; we have made it discussable and even put it into play with equally or hopefully stronger counter-arguments. Choice then becomes more possible.

Chapter 8 presents a list of commonly heard "pro-fessional rationalizations" in the business world and of-fers illustrations of individuals who crafted and delivered effective responses. Some of the most useful tools for identifying, deconstructing, and responding to these ra-tionalizations are outlined as well. Readers will come away from this chapter with a tool kit that can be used to address many of the most commonly encountered arguments for unethical business behavior, as well as exemplary stories of folks who did just that.

CHAPTER 9
PUTTING IT TO WORK

In this chapter, we return full circle to the stories from the Introduction—from the Giving Voice to Values initiative itself—to illustrate the power of the approach and to offer an invitation to be part of a growing cohort of peer coaches in business schools and business organizations who are practicing, mastering, and sharing this powerful thought experiment in ways that empower all of us to more fully, more often, and more effectively voice and act on our values.

## CHAPTER ONE

# Giving Voice to Our Values

## THE THOUGHT EXPERIMENT

A fundamental premise of many Eastern philosophies and martial arts is to move *with* one's momentum and energy, rather than fight against them. The approach to voicing and acting on our values described in these pages attempts to build on that same principle. Rather than taking a preaching stance wherein we might try to counter temptations with all the moral reasons why we should behave ethically, or taking a persuasive stance wherein we might counter those same temptations with all the practical arguments for ethical behavior, the approach here is to take an enabling stance. We try to identify both the times when we already want to act in accordance with our highest moral values and also the reasons why we feel that way, and then we focus on building the confidence and skills and the scripts that enable us to do so effectively and with the least amount of angst. Rather than pushing or pulling ourselves into values-based action, we try to grease the skids that might carry us there.

One way that we try to work with personal momentum, rather than fight against it, is by framing our discussion here as a thought experiment. We are invited to consider *how* we might voice and act on our values *if* we were going to do so. In this way, we sidestep all the pre-emptive arguments and rationalizations that pop up naturally, about how difficult or even impossible it may be to do so. We create a safe and enabling space, if you will, for experimentation and creative thinking.

In the service of creating that safe space, we try to be explicit about as many of the working assumptions that underlie this approach to enabling values-based action as possible. These assumptions are intended as the foundation for an exploratory rather than coercive stance. This explicit naming of our assumptions allows for a kind of informed consent at best, or at least for a provisional consent as we embark upon this experiment. Even if we are not entirely certain that we accept all of the assumptions, this provisional consent provides room for us to act *as if* we did, and to see where they might take us, thereby freeing us up to create scripts and implementation plans for values-driven actions that we might never otherwise develop. Then when we are faced with the actual decision to act on our values, we will at least have a well-developed strategy to consider. In this way, the default of non-action, or of just going along with the course of least resistance, will have a worthy counter position.

So in the service of this informed or provisional consent, let's consider the starting assumptions for Giving Voice to Values. These are twelve assumptions, or givens, that form the story line behind this approach to values-driven action.

## Assumption One: I want to voice and act upon my values.

As discussed in the Introduction, the fundamental assumption is that most of us want to find ways to voice and act on our values in the workplace, and to do so effectively. Interestingly, whenever ethical action in business is discussed, we often get stuck on the idea that even if we want to act ethically, we assume that many others do not. Therefore we conclude that our efforts will be for naught and, what's more, that we will likely pay a price for trying.

But why do we always focus on the folks who do not want to behave ethically? If we start instead from the premise that most of us would like to behave in accordance with our values, then it becomes less important whether everyone does so. Instead we only need "just enough" folks to share this position; it becomes simply a matter of critical mass. It is a glass-half-empty or half-full kind of issue. By starting from the assumption that most folks do want to voice and act on their best values, we begin to create that very possibility, because we eliminate one of the conclusions that prevent us from joining this group. (We are putting aside for a moment the question of which values we, or others, want to voice and act upon. That question is addressed in Chapter 2.)

Another objection to this first assumption may be the protestation: "But I might not want to act on my highest values in all situations!" However, just because an idea may not always be true does not mean it is never true. For the purpose of this thought experiment, we suppose that there are many times when we would indeed like to voice and act on our values, and by enabling that choice and learning to do so effectively, we are likely to expand the frequency of this choice. It becomes a genuine and even a realistic option for us.

### Assumption Two: I have voiced my values, at some points in my past.

Even though research and our own experiences reveal many individual and organizational inhibitors, most people have in fact chosen to voice and act on their values on some occasions. In conversations and interviews with managers at all levels of organizations and in the classrooms where this approach has been discussed, we have yet to find anyone who cannot think of times both when they have and when they have not done so. Typically this realization leads to a conclusion that no one is truly ethical. What if, as part of our thought experiment, we turned this around and concluded that no one is truly unethical? This conclusion can then be the foundation for building the muscle for more frequent and more effective values-driven actions.

## Assumption Three: I can voice my values more often and more effectively.

We have the potential to expand our capacity, our effectiveness, and our likelihood to voice and act on our values by acknowledging that we have such a choice, and by practicing what we would say and do if we made that choice.

The working metaphor for the Giving Voice to Values approach to values conflicts is that of an individual learning a new physical skill or sport. Not being an athletic type myself, I did once take a class in self-defense a number of years ago. The course was called Model Mugging, and the idea was that instead of simply learning the basic self-defense moves (fist to bridge of nose, heel to instep, knee to groin, and so on), we would also have the opportunity to experience the feel of a full-on blow directed at an instructor who was dressed in an entirely padded suit, like the Michelin Man. In this way, the students could practice delivering the various self-defensive moves full force, rather than simply talking about what action was called for or miming the moves in the air without the experience of impact on another human being. After practicing the moves full force in a supportive environment, we would have a chance to practice applying them during a simulated full-speed "attack" as well, with the same padded instructor.

The thinking and research behind this several-stage approach was that muscle memory is linked to both the experience of full-force contact as well as the heightened emotional state of the simulated engagement, and therefore, even if our brains are frozen or reacting slowly, our bodies would remember how to respond if we encountered that same emotional state again in an actual real-time situation.

There are several interesting aspects to this approach. Before engaging in the simulated attack, we first had to master the actual physical movements by breaking them down into their components and practicing them repeatedly, with full-force impact and with encouragement and feedback on our form. This is similar to the way a student of tennis or golf or any other sport might learn and practice the different strokes and positions and build the requisite muscle groups, as preparation for putting them together in actual play, or the way a musician practices playing or singing scales before attempting a complex musical composition.

So with GVV, the premise is that values-driven scripts and actions are a competency that can be learned, and that it is learned by both breaking it down into its component parts and by practicing the application of those components—scripts and action plans—in cooperative and lower-stress situations. Both the cognitive aspects of the process—analyzing the arguments and creating effective scripts—as well as the experiential aspects—actually saying the words in concert with peers who stand in as proxies for eventual workplace colleagues—are essential. In this way, we build the muscle and the muscle memory so that the approach will come more naturally and skillfully when we encounter actual values conflicts in real time.

Some might argue that this is simply an example of traditional role playing in the service of learning. On the contrary, although there is a value in the use of role playing, if we are immediately placed in a situation where we must voice our values in the face of an adversary who is primed to argue vehemently against our position, we may find ourselves unintentionally reinforcing those same anxieties and that same pessimism about our chances at success that we are trying to counter.

For example, too often participants in a role play of a values conflict will demonstrate their political astuteness, their savvy, and their experience with the so-called real world of business by assuming a skeptical, if not cynical, stance, pointing out all the reasons why a defense of ethical values is not realistic or practical. Such role plays tend to send the signal that values-based actions are naive, at best.

However, if instead of adversarial role plays, we create opportunities to practice our arguments in front of peers who assume the role of "coaches," we can work cooperatively and constructively to simultaneously reinforce the best of our arguments, to revise the weakest of our arguments, and to experience the physical and emotional act of voicing these arguments in public.

Of course, full-on adversarial role plays may still be helpful, but in order to avoid unintended negative reinforcement of our own best intentions, they would be used only after we have first taken the time to craft and actually practice speaking our positions in a collaborative context.

## Assumption Four: It is easier for me to voice my values in some contexts than others.

Developing the "muscle" for voicing our values does not diminish the importance of selecting and developing organizational cultures and policies and incentives that encourage such choices. In fact, our effort to promote the development of such cultures, policies, and incentives is, in itself, an instance of voicing values. And the more such organizational enablers are in place, the more likely it is that individuals will choose to voice their values. It is a kind of virtuous circle.

This is an important part of the puzzle, for there is much research that examines the impact for good or ill of organizational contexts that enable or disable "dissent" and that focus on narrowly defined versus broadly defined performance goals. We will discuss examples of this in subsequent chapters, but the important point here is to recognize that although the emphasis of the GVV approach is on the individual and his or her abilities and choices, the organization and its impact are not overlooked. Although GVV is an individual strategy, individuals operate within organizations that can limit or enhance the options available to address values conflicts.

Focusing on organizational pressures and norms is, again, not a reason to avoid voicing our values but rather another opportunity to reframe our choices and act on our values, this time by actually addressing the organizational context itself. As we will see, sometimes individuals can more effectively address values conflicts in the workplace by talking about what discourages ethical action and engaging colleagues in addressing those factors than by tackling the issue head-on. This becomes a kind of jujitsu move, where colleagues are engaged in "fixing" the organization in such a fashion that, by the way, addresses the values conflict itself. An example of this is when individuals focus on changing financial incentives and reporting systems that may not only enable, but also encourage, distortions in an organization's internal auditing. Looking for ways to fix the system in the service of more accurate planning and forecasting, along the way, addresses the distortions in reporting integrity.

### Assumption Five: I am more likely to voice my values if I have practiced how to respond to frequently encountered conflicts.

There are certain frequently heard "reasons and rationalizations" for not voicing and acting on our values. But there are also possible responses or reframings that we can use to counter these reasons and rationalizations. If we familiarize ourselves with these responses in advance, we are more likely to be able to access them when needed and potentially shift a conversation or change a mind. This is especially true when we begin to see that the types of reasons that we hear—and even offer ourselves—for not voicing our values tend to fall into a set of recognizable and limited categories, and therefore the levers for responding to them, or entirely recasting them, are similarly recognizable and consequently learnable.

Prior reflection on responses to values conflicts can also expand our confidence in the degrees of freedom we have in any given decision situation. That is, if we become "fluent" in ways to address the defenses of less than ethical behaviors, we will find ourselves more easily and more automatically doing so. Rather than experiencing that deer-in-headlights feeling when we confront values conflicts, our muscle memory can kick in and the emotionality of the moment is reduced.

I learned this lesson firsthand a number of years ago. While teaching at the Harvard Business School, I launched a research and course development project on Managing Diversity in the mid-1990s. There was no other course on the subject at the school then, but I had both an intellectual as well as a personal interest in pursuing this work. For a variety of reasons having to do with my own experiences and those of people I knew, I had always experienced significant discomfort when I witnessed unfairness or undeserved bias toward school or professional colleagues. Rather than anger toward the offender, however, I would tend to feel guilty and angry at myself for not being confident enough or skillful enough to counter the situation. At some level, I believe I felt that the experience of researching, constructing, and teaching a course on diversity might enable me to learn how to handle such situations myself, even as I was trying to teach others.

Although teaching the course was a very positive experience for me, at the end of the two years I felt that, sadly, I was no closer to that elusive sense of bulletproof confidence and skill that I believed I needed to be able to speak up when I witnessed unfairness in my professional life. I moved on to other projects. Less than a year later, however, while working as a consultant, I was led to reassess the impact of the diversity research and teaching I had done. Two situations in particular caught me up short.

In the first instance, my team was presenting a new piece of work to a potential client. The representative from the client's firm was making small talk at the start of our meeting, and he managed to make several joking but disparaging comments based on ethnic and class stereotypes. Although the comments were not specifically directed at me or any of my team members—who were racially diverse and included my boss as well as several more junior managers—I was concerned about the tone that we set for our ongoing working relationship. I didn't really think about it but I just heard myself suggesting, with calm but pointed good humor, that perhaps we should turn to topics about which we all were more informed. There was a palpable sense of relief among my colleagues, especially the more junior ones, and the client, unoffended, good-naturedly turned to a more appropriate topic. I was relieved, both because I did not want to lose the client but also because I did not want to bond with him on the basis of discriminatory humor.

In the second instance, I recognized that the senior member of my consulting team had made some incorrect and negative assumptions about the writing ability of the sole African-American junior member of our group. I don't believe this manager was intentionally biased, but his unconscious conclusion was barring the junior colleague from a plum assignment. I found myself in a car with this senior manager, and when the subject came up, I simply explained how impressed I was with the junior consultant's writing ability, providing concrete examples of this skill. As a result, the junior consultant received an attractive writing project, and I had the opportunity to work closely with him and benefit personally and professionally from the association.

I mention these two examples neither because I believe I handled them flawlessly nor to argue that I always counter bias when I see it. I still struggle with my desire to avoid conflict and with a certain natural reticence. However, I did manage to shift the behaviors and impacts on my peers in these two situations (not that I have any illusions that I actually changed the attitudes of the client in the first example). And I did so with a minimum of stress and hand-wringing on my own part. In fact, in both instances, I heard myself making comments that I would never have made prior to my diversity course. In fact, in the past, I would have felt horrible about both situations but would have likely remained tongue-tied.

I have concluded that the experience of researching and talking about the many ways that discrimination and bias can occur in professional contexts, and especially the identification of the many arguments against this type of bias and the many ways of responding to these situations, had had a profound impact on me. Not only had I seen how common such situations are, but I had also practiced, unwittingly, all the ways that one might respond. I was not shaken or put off my game when the circumstances arose. I was able to react calmly, thereby without signaling to my audiences that this was a "difficult" situation or that they were somehow "bad" people. The responses were fact-based, good-natured, and appropriate to the context. Had I been taken off guard or less prepared, I would likely have telegraphed more stress, emotion, and blame. But the funny part was, I had not known that I was so prepared until I was in these situations! So I revisited my assessment of the value of my research and discussions of diversity. I believe it was more effective than I had recognized. It was, in fact, a kind of pre-scripting.

## Assumption Six: My example is powerful.

Just as we ourselves would like to be able to voice and act on our values, we can assume that many of our colleagues would as well. If we can demonstrate credible responses to frequently heard reasons for not voicing and acting on our values, we may encourage and empower others to join us.

An undergraduate business student I interviewed was working in a plum internship doing research for a consulting firm. When her boss told her to lie about who she was to gain intelligence from a competitor, she explained that she didn't want to do so but that she would work to gather comparable information in other ways. Her boss, unconvinced by her ethical arguments, nevertheless indulged her alternative plan, and through hard work, the intern was able to generate a credible report without misrepresenting herself. It might be argued that she had had a very limited impact on the firm; after all, her boss was not likely to change his behavior going forward. However, the intern reported that later she was surprised and pleased to see that other interns began coming to her, asking how she managed to complete her task without deception because they, too, wanted to take that road. Whether the organization was changed or not, she felt that she had empowered some of her colleagues through her example. Additionally, rather than walking away from this internship with only a sense of disillusionment at what she had learned about how this reputable firm did business, she gained a sense of efficacy and greater confidence in her own options. In fact, she was offered an ongoing position with the firm.

### Assumption Seven: Although mastering and delivering responses to frequently heard rationalizations can empower others who share my views to act, I cannot assume I know who those folks will be.

The responses we develop and practice to frequently heard reasons and rationalizations for unethical behaviors are intended to strengthen our own confidence in voicing and acting on our values. Additionally, this practice can influence others who share our values conflict but are unable to find a way to explain their reluctance. However, we cannot assume we know who feels the conflict and who does not simply by observing their behavior because, as we have already acknowledged, we all have chosen to suppress these "felt" conflicts at some points in our past.

Thus, in the example above, the business student intern might have thought she had failed if her goal had been only to change her boss's behavior. However, unexpectedly and without her conscious intention, her behavior was noticed by some of her peers and they were influenced by her. This is important because often we can become discouraged from trying to voice our values because we are not certain of our ability to influence our intended audience. The thing is, we will experience more satisfaction from our efforts to voice our values if we remain open to the possibility of unintended positive impacts. This is not to say that we do not design our scripts and action plans with a careful eye to having a hoped-for impact on a particular audience; rather it is simply to acknowledge and value the additional or alternative positive impacts we may have.

The only real and ultimate control we have is over ourselves, which leads us directly to the importance of the next assumption.

### Assumption Eight: The better I know myself, the more I can prepare to play to my strengths and, when necessary, protect myself from my weaknesses.

The greater our self-knowledge, the more likely we are to be able to anticipate and manage our responses to values conflicts. Prior reflection on our own personalities and behavioral tendencies under pressure enables us to play to our strengths: that is, to frame the challenge we face in such a way that it draws on the skills and arguments with which we feel most adept and confident. Rather than accepting the challenge as it is put before us, we can take an active role in reshaping it.

This kind of self-assessment is not your typical values-clarification process. It is not about figuring out what is important to us; the Giving Voice to Values approach starts from the moment our values kick in. Instead this self-assessment is based on the observation that people who do act on their values often have found ways to describe the situation that give them power rather than ways that trigger their fear or feelings of inadequacy.

We can also use this self-knowledge as a preparation and trigger to consciously put mechanisms in place to protect us from our own weaknesses. However, research tells us that often these "mechanisms" need to go beyond mere self-knowledge and become external tools (incentives, deterrents, automatic review processes, transparency requirements, preestablished networks of sounding boards, et cetera). Our own internal awareness of our biases and tendencies is important but not enough to prevent us from falling prey to them: we need to go beyond awareness to active preparation for values-based decision making, a preparation that includes the scripting and action planning that GVV encourages.

### Assumption Nine: I am not alone.

When we encounter values conflicts in the workplace, often we feel isolated and personally at risk. We may assume that our peers will not share our concern, or that to raise the issue will polarize our colleagues or expose us to greater pressure and vulnerability. This may actually be true. However, interviews with individuals who have voiced their values in such situations reveal that, in most cases, they did find and rely upon some form of external support system.

The challenge is to identify whom to speak with and for which purposes. There are many different sources of support, both inside and outside organizations, and there are many ways of gathering support, some more direct than others. We can utilize our personal support networks (family, friends outside the organization) as sounding boards; we can reach out to our colleagues in the firm to build a coalition of allies or to gather supporting information; and we can engage in strategic use of the managerial hierarchy. However, we must consider carefully which approach is most appropriate in a particular situation, keeping in mind the implications not only for ourselves and the challenge we face, but also for the individuals we engage. The examples discussed here show different ways that individuals countered the tendency to feel isolated.

## Assumption Ten: Although I may not always succeed, voicing and acting on my values is worth doing.

When pursuing our values, just as with any other managerial action, we do not always succeed at what we set out to achieve, yet that does not necessarily prevent us and others from taking action. There are no guarantees or riskless action plans, around voicing values or anything else, and GVV does not claim that there are. Rather than backing off from our values because we can't muster the words or the strategies in the moment, and rather than rashly voicing values in ways that belie the management sophistication and interpersonal insight we would exhibit in a less charged situation, GVV is about providing the opportunity to hone and practice our approach, such that we feel greater confidence and can behave more skillfully. In this way, the goal is to increase the likelihood of success.

Additionally, we are more likely to voice our values if we have decided that the costs of not doing so, and the benefits of trying, are important enough to us that we would pursue them even though we cannot be certain of success in advance. In order to get to this place of clarity, we need to spend some serious time thinking about our own identity, our personal and professional purpose, and our definition of success and failure. We will explore each of those issues in the following pages.

However, it is also important to reflect clear-eyed upon the risks associated with voicing our values, so that we can be prepared to handle the possible implications.

### Assumption Eleven: Voicing my values leads to better decisions.

It is often difficult to be certain that a specific course of action is "right" or "wrong," but we are more likely to come to the best decision if we feel empowered to voice our concerns about values conflicts and discuss them with others. In fact, one of the most common objections to the idea of voicing and acting on our values is the concern that we may be wrong, that our values might spring from a place of self-righteousness or incomplete understanding. And of course, this is a valid concern.

Unfortunately, too often this concern serves to silence us, preventing us from sharing our perspectives because we assume that they are not valid. If, however, we learn to examine our values-based position in depth and from multiple perspectives, as the GVV approach outlines, we not only will become more adept at presenting our values-based position, but we will also be testing it against the views of others and supporting it with the necessary information. Our own position will become richer.

In addition, even if in the end we conclude that our going-in position was incorrect, the process of analyzing and sharing our concerns can improve our organizational decision-making process. In fact, one of the lessons shared by the individuals interviewed for GVV is that decisions are often improved if we do not assume that managerial directives are final and unquestionable, but rather view them as simply opening hypotheses. Taking this view can also help us to present our views with the calm confidence that comes from the belief that we are adding value by doing so.

## Assumption Twelve: The more I believe it's possible to voice and act on my values, the more likely I will be to do so.

We are more likely to voice and act on our values when we believe it is possible to do so, and to do so effectively. If we pay attention to positive examples of such voice and action and spend time developing support mechanisms and practicing the development and delivery of responses to frequently heard reasons and rationalizations for unethical actions, we can expand our sense of what's possible—another virtuous circle.

On the other hand, if we focus most of our time and attention identifying and bemoaning all the ways in which we are discouraged from voicing our values, we will be reinforcing that process. This is not only common sense; increasingly it is a phenomenon supported by research in the fields of positive psychology as well as the cognitive neurosciences.[1]

In fact, the GVV approach described in these pages is more than a set of insights and tools that we can learn to apply; the very act of reading and reflecting upon all the ways that folks have voiced and can act on their values can change the way we experience reality. That is, rather than proving that we can act on our values, we are simply making it true. And we do this by reframing the question from "*whether* to voice our values" to "*how* can we voice our values?"

Having now familiarized ourselves with the working assumptions behind the GVV thought experiment, it becomes important to ask: "What are our reactions to these assumptions?" If, as stated at the outset, our goal is to provide a space for an informed, or at least a provisional, consent to the GVV project, then it becomes important not only to name and define these underlying assumptions, but also to reflect on both our resonances with them as well as our reservations or objections to them. We might consider:

- Are there any of these assumptions that particularly resonate with us? Why?
- Are there any with which we disagree? Why?
- And if we disagree with any of them, how does that affect our attitude toward the effort to develop the scripts and skills and to practice voicing and acting on our values?

The important thing is not that we must accept all of these assumptions; the important thing is to be able to act "as if" we did for the purposes of this learning experience. By naming our agreement and resonances, we identify the assumptions we can rely on to bolster our confidence as we embark on the GVV experiment. And by naming our caveats and reservations, we can reduce the defensive need to resist the GVV experiment because we have not committed to anything other than an exploration process. We are simply acknowledging the possibility that we may be wrong about our caveats, or, stated positively, that the assumptions may be right.

As we work our way through the remaining chapters, we will see each of these assumptions illustrated and probed in the stories of individuals who have found ways to voice and act on their values. Finally, we will find that we have more leeway and power to create our own reality around voicing values than we may have assumed when we began this journey.

But first, before plunging more deeply into the process of voicing and acting on our values, it is useful to spend a bit of time defining our terms, and the next chapter explores just what we mean here when we talk about "values."

## CHAPTER TWO

# Values

## WHAT THEY ARE AND WHAT

## THEY ARE NOT

VALUES: Know and appeal to a short list of widely

shared values, such as honesty, respect,

responsibility, fairness, and compassion. In other

words, don't assume too little—or too much—

commonality with the viewpoints of others.

Before we go further it is important to explain what we mean here by the term "values," since this is obviously an overdetermined word. For example, how is our use of "values" the same as or different from "ethics" or "morals"? And further, when asked to name their values, many people, especially businesspeople, may include qualities like "innovation" or "creativity" or any number of other useful and important characteristics that do not even have an obvious moral dimension to them. So how do *those* values connect with our focus here, if they do? Although these different terms and even the multiple uses of the word "values" are often overlapping and used interchangeably, it is important to clarify our intent and usage in this book.

First of all, the focus here is on "values" rather than "ethics," because in general usage, ethics suggests a system of rules or standards with which one is expected to comply. That is, we may talk about business ethics, medical ethics, legal ethics, or more generally, professional ethics. Individual businesses often have their own formal codes of ethics (a set of written standards and guidelines); they distribute these widely and sometimes even conduct training sessions to make sure employees are aware of them. Thus, ethics is often seen as rule-based and externally imposed, something that exists outside the individual.

Furthermore, in the study of ethics, the emphasis is typically on models of ethical reasoning, such as deontology or duty-based ethics, utilitarian or consequentialist ethics, virtue ethics, and so on. The emphasis is therefore again on various external frameworks that can help us to discipline our thinking about various ethical choices and dilemmas. In particular, discussions of the application of ethical reasoning often focus on scenarios where the various models will lead us to different, conflicting decisions about what is "right," with a discussion of how we might try to resolve those tensions. For example, there are the classic hypothetical cases where we must choose between respecting the individual (duty-based ethics) and maximizing the good for the many (consequentialist ethics): Would we pull the railroad track switching lever if it would save the lives of many people in a train's path, but sacrifice the life of one individual on the alternative track?

This kind of analysis can be valuable in helping us consider the complexities of ethical dilemmas and teaching us to be rigorous and to recognize and question our own biases. However, it does not teach us how to enact those choices once made—which is the focus in this book. Ironically, this kind of analytic focus can actually have a dangerous unintended consequence, as was captured in the interview with a CEO that was mentioned in the Preface to this book.

As you will recall, this CEO described a freshly minted MBA's answer to his question about what he had learned in his business ethics course: "Well, first we learned about all the models of ethical reasoning—you know, utilitarianism, deontology, and so on—and then we learned that whenever you confront an ethical dilemma, you first decide what you want to do and then you select the model of ethical reasoning that will best support your choice."

Of course, this anecdote does not negate the importance of thinking rigorously about ethical challenges. But as the CEO had wanted to show me, the story does reveal an unanswered challenge in most efforts to talk about business ethics. Even in corporate settings where there is less emphasis on teaching models of ethical reasoning, the discussions will typically still revolve around considerations of what the "right thing" to do might be in a particular situation, rather than what to say and how to do it once you have decided the right course of action. People tend to walk away with a sense of confusion, at best, and a schooling in rationalizations (as was the case for that MBA student that our CEO interviewed), at worst.

So for all these reasons, we chose not to call our focus in these pages "Giving Voice to Ethics." Rather than the emphasis on externally imposed rules and sometimes seemingly sophistic reasoning exercises that are unfortunately associated with "ethics" education and training, we chose the word "values" because it suggests something that we own ourselves and hold dear—"*my* values"—and something that we experience deeply and internally, which, although it possesses a cognitive aspect, is not exclusively about analysis.

But what about the term "morals"? While morals and morality refer to standards of right and wrong conduct and this is certainly relevant to what we are talking about, again the word "morals" emphasizes the "rightness" or "wrongness" of a particular behavior more than how we feel about that behavior. That is, the emphasis is on judgment and discipline more than an affirmative pursuit of desired goals and objects. Admittedly, all of these terms overlap and the distinctions drawn here have as much to do with tone as substance, but that tone is important.

It is important because the fundamental stance we are taking in the Giving Voice to Values approach to values-driven action is one of alignment, of moving *with* our highest aspirations and our deepest sense of who we wish to be, rather than a stance of coercion and stern judgment, or of moving *against* our inclinations. Although self-discipline is certainly required to voice and act on our values, the emphasis here is on finding the part of ourselves that already wants to do this, and then empowering, enabling, training, and strengthening that self.

Finally, the word "value" refers to the inherent worth and quality of a thing or an idea, and we often talk about valuing a challenging job, a comfortable lifestyle, or even a well-made piece of clothing. However, the "values" we are discussing here are, in fact, values that most people would agree have a moral or ethical aspect to them. In this sense, these values are actually much the same as what we mean by "virtues." It's just that we are approaching them from a self-motivated aspirational stance, rather than a judgmental or self-disciplinary position. The word "value" is both a noun and a verb; it has inherent in it not only the concept of goodness—like "virtue"—but also the act of wanting, desiring, or personally "valuing" something. So the choice of the term "values" is about tone and positioning, as well as literal definition.

Now that we have settled on the term "values," the question becomes what values? And whose values? When asked to list our "core" values, we will certainly encounter disagreements about the items on the list and their relative priorities. However, I always find it instructive when groups are invited to participate in values clarifications exercises. If the values people are invited to choose among include many items that do not carry an inherently moral aspect—like a comfortable lifestyle (for example, the well-made clothes mentioned above) or even more profound concepts such as access to the natural world, creativity or dependability, independence or community—there will be a lot of disparity among the priority lists that individuals generate. On the other hand, if they are invited to identify their core moral or ethical values, the lists often tend to converge.

Much research has been done over time and across cultures, and although differences do surface, what is important to remember here is that there is a great deal of commonality among the lists of moral or ethical values that most individuals identify as central, and that this shared list is rather short. For example, in *Moral Courage: Taking Action When Your Values Are Put to the Test,* Rushworth Kidder describes the extensive areas of consensus on core values he finds in his own cross-cultural surveys, as well as in the research of others.[1] The influential psychologist Martin Seligman writes: "There is astonishing convergence across the millennia and across cultures about virtue and strength. . . . Confucius, Aristotle, Aquinas, the Bushido Samurai Code, the Bhagavad-Gita, and other venerable traditions disagree on the details, but all of these codes include six core virtues."[2]

These virtues are wisdom, courage, humanity, justice, temperance, and transcendence.[3] Drawing from his own research, Kidder identifies a similar, more simply put, list of five widely shared values: honesty, respect, responsibility, fairness, and compassion.[4]

Similarly, in the development of their Integrative Social Contracts Theory, Thomas Donaldson and the late Thomas W. Dunfee posit a set of hypernorms that can guide conflict resolution in economic activities when working across diverse groups. They argue that

> global macrosocial contractors. . . would not necessarily deny the existence of a thin universal morality, nor of principles so fundamental that, by definition, they serve to evaluate lower-order norms. Defined in this way and reaching to the root of what is ethical for humanity, precepts we choose to call "Hypernorms" should be discernible in a convergence of religious, political, and philosophical thought, or at least it is a reasonable hope that we should discern such a convergence. The concept of a hypernorm is used to establish the boundaries of moral free space, and individual hypernorms would limit the imposition of ethical obligations within a given microsocial community. We call such principles "hypernorms" because they represent norms by which all others are to be judged.[5]

Although we may quibble around the edges, knowing that, in general, a certain brief list of values is widely shared gives us both a useful (because of its commonality) and manageable (because of its brevity) foundation that we can appeal to when trying to address values conflicts in the workplace. Recognizing that our differences or disagreements about values, though real, do not preclude the development and pursuit of *shared goals* is a helpful primary position to adopt when we think about how to voice and act on those values.[6]

Accepting this premise—that is, the existence of a short list of shared values and, therefore, the possibility of shared goals—enables us both to prioritize our differences and also to frame the most important ones in ways that are more likely to communicate and resonate with different audiences. We will be able to see both others as well as ourselves more clearly, more objectively, because we have made the effort to distinguish between those values that are most universal and those that are more context-specific. This is not to suggest that a context-specific value is not important, but rather that it may be helpful to understand its link to a particular history and situation, and therefore understand its apparent relevance or lack thereof for those embedded in different histories and situations. And when we believe that a value is important enough and needs to be enacted and voiced, we can look for ways to express its link to that short list of values held in common across different contexts.

Perhaps some illustrations would be helpful here.

Near the end of a recent lecture and discussion about Giving Voice to Values with a group of graduate business school students and business leaders, one MBA student spoke up. Her comment went something like this: "I am from India and the norms and practices of business there are different. In my work experience, I found that it was often impossible to voice and act on my values because certain less than honest or ethical practices are just accepted." The woman appeared irritated, even angry. Rather than directly countering her reality, her experience of the futility of voicing values in an Indian business context, I invited her to share more about her own experiences, why she had drawn this conclusion, and how she had dealt with it.

She went on to talk about her discomfort with certain business practices in her previous employment situation, as well as about a time when she herself had purchased a used computer that was guaranteed to be in working order but turned out to be defective. She talked about how offended she was by this violation of business integrity. And she concluded her remarks by saying that, given the futility of trying to enact her values in the workplace in her home country, instead she, in her free time, focused her energy on working with a nonprofit organization that addressed some of the social and economic problems in her community.

The explicit point she was making was that acting on our values is context-specific, particularly across cultures. The implicit point was a sort of justification of her own choice not to try to fight the particular business practices she had faced before coming to business school. There seemed an inherent contradiction here. On one hand, she was saying she had no choice, but on the other, she felt the need to justify the choice she had made.

In trying to respond to the woman's comments, it seemed important to find a way to recognize and strengthen her view of herself as, in fact, having had— and still having—a choice about how to respond to her context. But this had to be done without locking her into a perception of herself as a fundamentally unethical person precisely because she may not have always done so. Obviously this was tricky. Arguing that she did in fact have choices in her prior business roles might reinforce her self-perception as an unethical person and might therefore lead her to feel disempowered and defeated when confronting future conflicts; on the other hand, simply reassuring her that she really had no choice after all could fuel the kind of self-justifying biases—for example, her generalization that it is impossible to behave ethically in Indian business—that could make it easier to overlook or rationalize future failures to act.

However, the seeds of a response to her argument were embedded in this woman's own comments. She clearly did, in fact, experience the less than honest business dealings she described as a values conflict. On a professional level, she acknowledged that the behaviors of some businesses at home were less than ethical; on a more personal level, she felt offended and cheated by the computer dealer who sold her a defective machine. So the first response to her comments was simply to reflect back to her that she obviously was a person with active values.

Second, I suggested that the fact that she did experience values conflicts, at a minimum, complicated her assertion that the norms and business context in India were less than ethical. That is, without denying or oversimplifying contextual differences, she herself—an Indian national—had demonstrated that such generalizations are not universal.

Third, once her cultural assumptions had been thus complicated, it was helpful to point out that such contextual pressures to behave unethically are not unique to India. In fact, most folks confronting difficult values conflicts in the workplace are able to point to a story of explicit or implicit organizational or cultural norms that are less than ethical and that make the conflict more difficult. For example, the salesperson who gives inappropriate "gifts" to a customer in order to secure a contract will argue that this is the unstated norm of the industry. The manager who adjusts the quarterly statement to transfer past expenses forward or unreceived revenues backward will explain that this sort of "smoothing" is standard operating procedure and is actually an expected behavior. And organizational behavior research is rife with examples of the implicit and explicit pressures and norms of socialization that lead to unethical behavior.[7] I cited these examples not with the intent to negate the power of the pressures this Indian woman experienced, but rather to suggest that they are not unique to one culture, industry, or function, and that, in fact, people sometimes find ways to counter them.

Fourth, her story about her work with a community nonprofit demonstrates that she is the kind of person who can and does act on her values. The trick was to reflect this reality back to her in a way that suggested that she had effectively found ways to counter widespread problems and challenges in one part of her life, thereby raising the possibility of seeing herself as the kind of person who might do so in other areas as well.

If I had directly countered her assertion that it was impossible to act on her values in India, I would have run the risk of pushing this woman into a self-defeating insistence on her own powerlessness and on my lack of understanding of her culture. Instead I asked her to share more of her own story, revealing the complexity of her own feelings and past behaviors. In this way, she felt invited to see herself as a person of values, and specifically an Indian person of values; to reflect on the ways she had acted on her own values in the past; and to recognize that if she feels and acts in these ways, there may be others in her business context at home who may feel and act in these ways as well.

Clearly this discussion did not resolve the question of exactly what she could or would do in the future when she encountered such values conflicts in the workplace, but she left the discussion engaged and positive. Her demeanor had changed and her facial expression cleared and relaxed; she was even smiling. She was one of the first to come up to talk about next steps after the discussion ended and she became engaged in an external (and hopefully also internal) dialogue about her real options.

Her conflicts had become "speakable" in a different way. Before, she had felt torn between anger at the injustice and lack of ethics she observed in her culture and a sense of futility at the idea that this might have something to do with India—or by extension, with herself as an Indian national. After this discussion, no longer was the fact of being Indian, or of working in an Indian business, necessarily a barrier. One of the keys to this reframing of her self-image and her view of her business context was the recognition of some values that she and presumably others in the Indian business context might share. Since this conversation, it has been exciting to see that some of the most enthusiastic business faculty adopters of the Giving Voice to Values approach have been in India. Some of these professors are collecting stories of Indian managers who have in fact found ways to voice and act on their values, despite pressures to the contrary, and they are developing them into case study examples.[8]

I shared the example above because whenever I talk about Giving Voice to Values, there are two questions that inevitably come up. First of all, someone in the audience will typically remark that this approach must be culturally specific, and that it could not possibly work in all parts of the world. Sometimes that question comes from someone who is actually a citizen of a country where she or he feels such an approach would be challenging. That is the example above. More frequently, however, the comment is raised by someone who is talking about a part of the world that he or she believes would be inhospitable to GVV. Sometimes this person will have lived or conducted research in that part of the world; other times they simply assume that GVV must be culturally specific either because actually speaking up will run counter to the culture in some places or because, despite the research noted above about shared values, they just don't believe that common ground can be found.

Let's look at these two issues separately. The concern about whether the act of "speaking up" will be culturally feasible provides a good opportunity to note that the words "giving voice" are intended metaphorically here. That is, although we may sometimes assume that voicing our values means standing up and giving an impassioned little speech against injustice or dishonest practices, in reality the stories encountered and the examples described in this book are much more varied and nuanced than that.

Giving voice may mean simply asking the well-framed and well-timed question that allows people to think in a new way about a situation. Or it may mean working to make sure that certain information is included in a proposal that allows decision makers to see longer-term or wider potential impacts for their choices than originally considered. It may mean speaking quietly, behind the scenes, with someone who is better positioned than we are to raise an issue. Or it may mean simply finding another, ethically acceptable way to accomplish an assigned task. We will see examples of all these approaches in the following pages, but the point here is that "giving voice" can be seen as a metaphor for finding a way to embody and enact our values, but it might not mean actually "speaking up" in the ways we usually conceive of that.

The other concern is that values may differ so much across cultures that common ground will remain elusive, thereby invalidating one of the premises of GVV—that is, that we do have some vital shared values. Notwithstanding research and experience that describe real differences in priorities, preferences, and communication styles across cultures, as well as the research noted previously about the broadly shared but brief list of common values across cultures, let me tell another story that illustrates the approach here. Recently I was invited to share the GVV approach with a university in the United Arab Emirates, the American University of Sharjah. Several members of the business faculty there were quite intrigued and offered to pilot one of the exercises with their students, as the basis for further, customized curriculum development. As part of this effort, they collected stories from students about times when they did and did not voice and act on their values, and I had the opportunity to read these stories before my visit and work with the faculty and students on site.[9]

Although the student body at this institution is quite diverse, with more than eighty countries represented, over half of the students come from Arab nations. One of the concerns that many of the faculty members— many of whom were expatriates—expressed to me was that often their Arab students did not share the same values as the faculty concerning the inappropriateness of cheating in their academic work (and presumably in their wider lives). These professors wanted to be understanding of cultural norms but also to establish some ground rules for fairness across students in grading. As for myself, this was my first visit to any Arab nation and I was curious to see whether the GVV approach would be useful in this context. I tried to approach the encounter as an experiment, because I was quite aware of my inexperience and wanted to keep an open mind.

As I read the student papers, however, I was struck by the power of the personal revelations and felt a strong connection with the student authors even though many of their experiences were beyond my ken: discrimination against Indian nationals; arranged marriages; religious censorship. And I found a lot of commonality in the actual values discussed, even when the specific contexts differed. With regard to the cheating question, though, I was struck by a student who wrote about being asked by a close friend to provide answers during a final exam. The student said that he did not condone cheating and admitted that his decision to help his friend conflicted with his own personal position on academic honesty.

However, he went on to talk about all the kinds of rationalizations that one typically hears, about what was at stake for his friend; about how he might have felt better able to stand up if the friend had not been so close to him; about how he would have preferred to help his friend to study for the test rather than to provide answers during the actual exam; and so on.

What struck me about this story, and many of the others, was that although the student may have ultimately been trying to justify a decision to cheat, the reasons offered were not that cheating was not wrong, but rather that it was in conflict with other values like loyalty or with the realities of peer pressure. In the end, this is no different from the kinds of justifications and explanations that we hear for cheating elsewhere. It seemed useful to point this out, not only to the faculty who had expressed concern that their students viewed cheating as acceptable, but to the students themselves in a public presentation. Just because we may violate a value does not mean that we would not like to uphold it, if we felt we could find a way to do so effectively. And just as realizing that her experiences with less than ethical business behavior did not mean that all Indians were unethical helped to empower the student described earlier, expressing the values conflict around cheating can help reveal to the faculty as well as to the students in Sharjah that there is, in fact, a shared respect for academic integrity that they can work to build upon, in an effort to reduce cheating behaviors.

Providing the opportunity to express one's values, to identify the arguments that we typically hear—and offer—for our own behaviors when they conflict with these values, and then beginning to brainstorm about how one might reframe the situation is what GVV is all about. The student who described the cheating dilemma was already beginning to understand that in the future, he or she might respond to the request for exam answers by offering instead to help the friend study in advance, for example. The student's paper also revealed the inherent contradiction between helping a friend because he or she is close, on one hand, and the fact that a close friend would presumably not want to put another in a situation that was so difficult and conflicted.

Again, although these recognitions do not make the decisions easy, they do allow the individual student to begin to see himself or herself as someone who would like to avoid cheating and who is looking for a way to do so, and they allow the faculty to view their students in the same way. This provides a much broader common ground to stand upon than if students viewed themselves as fundamentally unethical because they gave in to their friend and if professors viewed their students as holding fundamentally alien value sets from themselves. Such views discourage the effort to brainstorm solutions and empower actions before it starts. Interestingly, the only professor from an Arab nation I spoke with in Sharjah talked about the importance of discouraging cheating and about how he tried to support his daughter, a college student herself, when she tried to resist pressures from her classmates. Clearly, the concern about integrity was not an exclusively "Western" idea.

When talking across cultures, rather than beginning with a position that we believe to be right and then asking (insisting?) that others agree with it, it is helpful to begin by asking about the other person's values. In Sharjah, I asked folks to tell us about the times when they felt they were asked or expected to behave in ways that conflicted with their values, and how they handled it. In this way, we begin from a position of expecting and respecting values in the individual with whom we are trying to connect. Right from the start, we found shared values to build upon.

Another cultural comparison can be found in the Aspen Institute Business and Society Program's MBA student attitude surveys mentioned in the Introduction to this book. Aspen BSP has been conducting these surveys since 2001, and the most recent, from 2008, not only surveyed fifteen business schools in the United States, Canada, and the United Kingdom but also conducted a comparable survey of fourteen business schools in China.[10] Although there were some differences, the major findings from the Western schools and those in China were quite similar in many areas.

Graduate students in both surveys tend to report that, although corporate responsibility to society is important, they see the primary benefit that companies gain from such good citizenship as being reputational, as opposed to direct positive impact on the bottom line. Students in both surveys report that work-life balance and compensation will be among their top three priorities in post-MBA job selection. Western students rated "challenging and diverse job opportunities," "compensation," and "work-life balance" as most important, in that order. Chinese students rated "compensation," "opportunities for training and development," and "work-life balance" as most important, with "challenging and diverse job opportunities" a close fourth.

When asked what they would do if they found that their values conflicted with those of their companies, the Western and the Chinese respondents differed somewhat in the tactics they selected, but the lowest answer in both groups (less than 10 percent reported "very likely") was that they would "not mind too much" if they encountered such values conflicts. Although the survey questions were highly general, the findings were encouraging with regard to the ability to find some common foundations for discussions of values-based management. Strategies for addressing values conflicts (speaking up for oneself, trying to get others to join in, and so on) may differ, and more Chinese students reported that they would "quietly handle the stress," but the issue itself appears to be significant for both groups. And importantly, this supports the primary assumption behind the Giving Voice to Values approach: that is, most of us would like to be able to find ways to voice and act on our values. Finally, and interestingly, women students report a greater concern about the social performance of business than do men among both the Western and the Chinese schools surveyed.

The other big question that people invariably ask on first hearing about Giving Voice to Values goes something like this: "I really like the idea of actually preparing folks—myself and others—to speak about and act on their values, giving them the chance to script and practice their voice. But what if their values are wrong? Aren't we just empowering folks to be more skillful at arguing for unethical positions?" This is a very important question.

After careful consideration, I have become comfortable with my response, and let me share it with you here. The reality is that we already do spend a great deal of time practicing and pre-scripting the reasons and rationalizations for *not* acting on what we think is right. Even as children we instinctively defend our misbehavior when we are caught: "Everybody else does it!" or "Jimmy made me do it!" or "I didn't know!" We become quite adept at explaining away our transgressions when we want to do so.

However, the focus in this book is on the times when we do not want to transgress, when we actually want to find ways to voice and act on our values. Our working hypothesis is that if we are able to adhere to our values in those instances when we are already motivated to do so, the working world will be greatly different. It's not that all bad actors really want to do good; rather it's that *some* of us do, some of the time, and that empowering us in these moments will realign the workplace reality.

So if your concern is that by learning to voice our values, we might be empowering the wrong values, I respond by saying that those "wrong" values are already empowered. The goal here is to raise the volume and increase the sophistication of those arguments that are less often heard, that are less practiced, and that can transform the workplace conversation.

The fact is that the reasons for doing "good" are often based on rules and precepts—those ethical codes we talked about earlier—while the reasons for less than ethical behavior are usually couched in more immediate and concrete arguments: your bonus will be bigger or, perhaps more uncomfortably, if you resist you will ensure that the bonuses of your peers will be smaller! On the contrary, arguments for ethical behavior often rely on an appeal to longer-term costs, less immediate benefits, and more intangible goods.[11] For all these reasons, these arguments often come a bit less easily to the tongue and require more forethought and pre-scripting.

But, you may counter, just because our position is based in a belief that we are doing right, that doesn't ensure that we are doing right. And I respond that if we learn to raise and express these values clearly and confidently, even if our original values-based position were to prove wrong, wouldn't the discussion itself be a positive thing in your organization? Wouldn't it be a good thing that you and your peers had to think through the decision at hand? And even if your position is ultimately proven incorrect, wouldn't it be a good thing that you felt truly heard and had the chance to see the organizational decision as correct, rather than as something you sheepishly complied with, believing all the while that you were doing wrong?

Fundamentally, GVV is about empowering anyone and all of us to voice positions that derive from a sense of doing right, with the assumption that such an impetus is important to express and consider, and that strengthening this impetus in and of itself is worthwhile. In the end, none of us can be certain in all situations what the right thing to do is, but I believe we can agree that it is important to try to find and act on that "right" and that empowering voice will move us forward in that endeavor.

## CHAPTER THREE

# A Tale of Two Stories

## THE POWER OF CHOICE

CHOICE: Discover and believe you have a choice
about voicing values by examining your own
track record. Know what has enabled and
disabled you in the past, so you can work with
and around these factors. And recognize, respect,
and appeal to the capacity for choice in others.

Earlier in the Introduction we asked, "Is there free will in business?" In the context of this book, the most useful answer is that *free will is a matter of free will.* That is, as we saw in the essays written by MBA students, when encountering similar challenges some folks believed and acted as if they had a choice, and others did not. Of course, the circumstances in any two situations are never entirely equivalent, but the fact is that, even in those examples where individuals reported that they did, in fact, voice and act on their values, they had colleagues in those same organizations who did not. That is, there were people in the same organizations and situations who were making different choices about speaking up.

Our intent here is not to conclude that those who spoke up were necessarily better, braver, or more competent people than those who did not. Rather, we want to consider these questions:

- Do we think that those individuals who told stories of speaking and acting on their values may have ever encountered a values conflict where they did not do so?
- Do we think that those individuals who told stories of not speaking up may have ever encountered a values conflict when they did speak and act on their values?

The answer to each of these questions, I suspect, will be "yes." And this is probably the strongest evidence we can bring to bear on this subject of choice—we know we have choice because we ourselves have exercised it. So the question then becomes, why do we choose to voice and act on our values when we do? And how can we build the confidence and skills and determination to do so more often?

As mentioned earlier, the responses to our questions about values conflicts in interviews with managers and business students were surprising. When they were invited to describe a time when they experienced a values conflict in the workplace and how they handled it, many of them seemed eager to describe both the times when they had, as well as the times when they had not, voiced and acted on their values. The question triggered an examination of the different choices they had made, and an exploration of why they may have made them. It seemed that interviewees did not want to contribute to a sense that these choices are easy, or always obvious, or that they themselves were somehow immune to the pressures of the situations. They described these complexities not as a means to rationalize or defend their choices, but rather as a form of self-reflection and honesty. The interviews themselves seemed an opportunity to learn about their own strengths, motivations, and inherent tendencies. It seems that we are neither as good nor as bad, neither as strong nor as weak, as we may have assumed.

Recognizing the fact that we are all capable of speaking and acting on our values, as well as the fact that we have not always done so, is both empowering and enlightening. It is perhaps the most important of the ways of thinking about values in the workplace we want to share in this book. It opens a path to self-knowledge, as well as situational analysis, that we may otherwise short-circuit. And by looking through this particular lens of "choice," we will see that each of the other ways of thinking and tools discussed here is helpful only once we have chosen to use it in the service of our values. In fact, many of the tools discussed here, such as reframing decisions, can be values-neutral: that is, they can be used by anyone to pursue any goal. They can be used for good or ill. It is our choice to try to answer the question—"How can I speak and act on my values in this situation?"—that is the essential first step.

So in the service of this exploration, we have designed a self-reflection exercise called "A Tale of Two Stories." And although this exercise has now been used in many business educational settings around the world, from undergraduate and MBA classrooms to executive training programs, it is also a perfect starting point for *individuals* who want to build their ability to voice and act on their values. It has proven extremely powerful as a way to frame our decision to voice and act on our values as a matter of confidence and skill, as much or more than as a matter of our "goodness" as individuals. The exercise itself is a useful starting point for building this confidence and skill, because it requires us to look, clear-eyed and honestly, at who we are, who we have been, and who we can be—at our best as well as at our less than best. Instead of focusing on preaching or efforts to persuade ourselves and others to behave ethically, the focus becomes one of action planning and scripting. Rather than an exhortation to be other than who we are, the exercise is positioned as a tool to help us be who we want to be, and therein lies its usefulness.

So let me offer a bit of a disclaimer here. The ideas we have gathered in our interviews, research, and piloting of the Giving Voice to Values approach are not rocket science. If you are reading this, you have already understood the heart of it, which is the thought experiment—asking not what is the right thing to do, but rather how can we get the right thing done—and the basic insights garnered from thoughtfully engaging in the two-stories exercise. The rest of this book is a sharing of the observations, the tools, and the tips generated from work with this approach over the past few years.

So as always with GVV, we begin this exercise from the assumption that most of us want to bring our "whole selves" to the workplace, and to act in accordance with our deepest values and commitments.[1] Yet research and experience tell us that we will frequently encounter values conflicts in our careers, when our values and purpose—the way we want to live and work—seem unaligned with the expectations of bosses, clients, peers, or the wider organization. This exercise is designed to help us identify and develop the competencies necessary to work on that alignment, by reflecting on our previous experiences—successful and less so—of voicing and acting on our values in the workplace and by uncovering the conditions and problem definitions that have empowered us in the past to effectively voice our values, as well as those which tend to inhibit this action.

The exercise is simple. First, recall a time in your work experience when your values conflicted with what you were expected to do regarding a particular, nontrivial management decision, and you spoke up and acted to try to resolve the conflict in a way that was consistent with your values.[2] After describing the situation briefly, consider and answer the following four questions:

1. What did you do, and what was the impact?
2. What motivated you to speak up and act?
3. How satisfied are you? How would you like to have responded? (This question is not about rejecting or defending past actions but rather about imagining your ideal scenario.)
4. What would have made it easier for you to speak and act?
   • Things within your control?
   • Things within the control of others?

After responding to these questions—the first story—we then invite the second story: recall a time in your work experience when your values conflicted with what you were expected to do regarding a particular, nontrivial management decision, and you did *not* speak up and act to try to resolve the conflict in a way that was consistent with your values. After describing the situation briefly, consider and answer the following four questions:

1. What happened?
2. Why didn't you speak up and act? What would have motivated you to do so?

3. How satisfied are you? How would you like to have responded? (Again, this question is not about rejecting or defending past actions but rather about imagining your ideal scenario.)
4. What would have made it easier for you to speak and act?
   - Things within your control?
   - Things within the control of others?

The power of this exercise lies in both the realities it unmasks and the myths that it defuses. The lessons are both individual and organizational; strategic and tactical; cognitive and emotional. The juxtaposition of the two stories and our answers to the reflection questions enables us to define both our individual motivators and inhibitors as well as the organizational motivators and inhibitors that affected us. In fact, part of this exercise focuses on identifying a list of "enablers" and "disablers" that affect our ability and willingness to voice our values.

So what are some of the lessons from this exercise that have surfaced from its use in settings as diverse as the MBA Orientation at the Massachusetts Institute of Technology in Cambridge to a required Business Ethics class at INSEAD in France to an Operations Management and an Organizational Behavior class at the American University of Sharjah to an executive Leadership Development program at the University of California in Los Angeles, and beyond?

To begin with, this is decidedly not an easy exercise. Folks typically need some time to really reflect in order to come up with examples of each type of situation. This can be due to several factors. First of all, if we feel we have not acted on our values, there is sometimes a tendency to push those memories to the back of our minds. It is not comfortable to dwell on them because they clash with a view of ourselves as basically good people. Of course, if we do not reflect on these situations, we may be doomed to repeat them, or to succumb to an overly positive self-image that blinds us to our own self-justifying rationalizations and to the real impacts of our choices.

But it is extremely important that we juxtapose these memories with the times when we have, in fact, acted in accordance with our highest aspirations, so that we do not go to the other extreme and surrender to an entirely negative and self-defeating view of ourselves. This exercise walks us along a fine line, finding realism in the balance between a negative and an approving view of our past behaviors. In fact, this duality becomes the source of motivation and energy for future action. We become neither discouraged nor self-satisfied, but rather both concerned and encouraged.

The examples themselves tend to fall into several broad categories. Typically there are three types of stories that emerge: there are stories of "wrongs" that we have been asked or directed to perform (misrepresent billable hours, tamper with financial reports, overstate the abilities of a team or a product, et cetera); there are stories of "wrongs" done to others that we have witnessed and about which we had to decide whether or not to intervene (discriminatory or unfair treatment, misrepresentation of facts, and so on); and there are stories of "wrongs" that have been done by others to ourselves (for example, discriminatory or unfair treatment).

When I first started sharing this exercise, I was disappointed at the stories that fell into the third category, wrongs done to ourselves. I thought that this was a bit of a cop-out and that it indicated that folks were not truly engaging in a deep and honest self-reflection. However, I began to see in subsequent discussion that personalizing the "wrong" was an effective path into the discussion for some who might be a bit more uncomfortable with immediately admitting to wrongdoing toward another. Rather than immediately alienating these individuals, or causing them to conclude that the discussion was irrelevant to them, it was important to give them a chance to ease into it. Typically once they begin to hear the stories shared by others, they can open up a bit more. Additionally, I began to recognize that being able to speak up about a wrong done to myself takes a kind of courage and certainly requires a set of skills similar to those needed to speak up in the other circumstances. And for those who may be skeptical about discussions of values in the workplace, this is a way of demonstrating the direct personal value of the endeavor.

Often in debriefing this exercise, since we reflect on the times when we have voiced our values first, by the time we begin to think about the time when we failed to do so, we are viewing it through the lens of empowerment. That is, we begin to reflect on how we might have—at best—transformed the "disablers" into "enablers" of values-based action, or at least neutralized them. So it might be useful to begin to share some of the enablers and disablers that we typically uncover.

So let us consider the enablers by asking: what would have made it easier to speak and act? As we review the list that follows, we will see that by identifying the enablers, several other things tend to happen. First, we will see that the disablers are often simply the absence or the reverse of the enablers; and second, identifying an enabler triggers a reflection on how we can bring it into being. That is, we begin to realize that we are not passive victims of the situation we confront.

Finally, reflecting on enablers and disablers reveals that some of them are widely and commonly shared among most of us. That is, most of us are more comfortable when we are not alone in our positions, for example (referring to the first enabler below, "allies"). However, some enablers and disablers are truly unique to our own personalities. For example, there are some folks who actually become motivated and empowered when they feel that they are the "lone voice" for a crucial position. They actually enjoy the position of being perceived as the contrarian. If this is true for us, then it suggests that we might be more likely to voice values when we can frame them as high stakes and when we can see ourselves as the lone and necessary champion—and the GVV approach is all about framing a decision in a way that it appeals to and brings out the best in ourselves. After all, the act of framing is itself another choice.

For all of these reasons, the act of enumerating what enabled us to voice our values when we did, and what disabled us from doing so when we did not, is a fruitful exercise. That is, we identify positive conditions that we can strive to create or simulate; we can identify ways to transform negative conditions; and we can identify aspects of our own personalities and characters to which we can play in order to strengthen our likelihood and ability to enact our values.[3] The following pages enumerate the most prevalent enablers and disablers we find.

## Allies

It is typically easier to voice and act on our values when we do not feel alone. Sometimes allies are within the organization, but in some cases individuals find support and sounding boards in friends, family members, or people who work in similar positions at other organizations. In extreme situations, this ally may be a consulted attorney or an outside expert. Obviously, in all cases, folks need to attend to issues of confidentiality, and sometimes that means sharing a very limited, disguised, or even hypothetical version of the issue at hand.

The point is, however, that rather than simply engaging in the so-called *Wall Street Journal* test—that is, imagining how we would feel if others knew about our decision—we actually talk, out loud, to someone else about it.[4] This is, in fact, the single most striking difference we found in our reading of the hundreds of stories shared by those MBA students who wrote about facing values conflicts, as explained in the Introduction. The students who found ways to enact their values had said something, at some point, out loud and to someone outside their own heads. This single act makes the decision feel more real, less hypothetical, less easily avoided. We have brought it into the light.

And as soon as individuals begin to talk about it, the fact is, they are not alone anymore. In other words, although the absence of allies is often identified as a reason why we do not voice our values, the stories people tell demonstrate that allies can be found and even created. Often allies are themselves a matter of choice. As we will see in some of the stories later in this book, some people found allies by simply asking for opinions from others in the organization: Have you ever encountered this type of situation? Have you seen others handle such a situation? Or even, have you ever seen someone handle such a situation differently? In other words, sometimes we have to ask for what we want to hear, rather than simply asking for what the assumed path of least resistance might be. Lisa Baxter (whose story is recounted in Chapter 7) explains that one of her most important enablers was the decision not to assume that opinions or preferences expressed by her bosses were orders. Rather she chose to see them as the opening gambit for discussion and exploration. She created allies at best, or thought partners at least, from the very people who had presented her with the values conflict.

Reviewing the many accounts produced by the "tale of two stories," we have collected a set of insights and tools to respond to the need for allies. First, know who you are and whether you are one of those individuals who actually enjoy and are motivated by identifying as a sort of "lone ranger" pursuing a values-driven position, or whether you are one of the far larger group of people who feel much more comfortable with a network of allies by your side.

If you are among the latter group, consider how you might create your own network, *in advance* if you are responding to the kind of values conflict that will be endemic and repeated in your industry or your position, or *at the time of the choice,* if it is a more unexpected and one-off type of conflict. In some cases, this is simply a matter of asking the kinds of questions mentioned above. In other situations, it may mean looking outside your organization for networks of individuals who care about the same issue. In the case of purchasing director Felipe Montez, this meant looking for external coalitions of companies and NGOs that were working on the same issues of human rights and worker safety in global supply chains that he was confronting.[5] The very act of talking to others who share our concern helps us to see beyond the pressures of our own context.

Depending on the urgency and scope of the issue, sometimes it is necessary to build a network of allies over time, as we gain their trust. As we will see, Lisa Baxter and Denise Foley (Chapter 6) built trusting and respectful relationships with their organizational superiors over a series of experiences. Their most important allies needed to be cultivated.

## Selection and Sequencing of Audiences

Interestingly and often self-defeatingly, we sometimes tend to focus so much on the ethical aspects of voicing our values that we neglect or even seem to think it is somehow crass to focus on effective communication skills. However, stories of those who enacted their values are full of careful planning, skillful scripting, and adroit choreography.

For example, it is critically important to think carefully not only about to whom we raise our values concerns but also about to whom we speak first. Just as selecting the audience who actually has decision-making authority is an important enabling factor in effectively voicing our values, it can be a disabler if that audience is blind or deaf to our entreaties.

When we need to convince our boss that a recommended course of action is not the right one, sometimes it is useful to consider the person or persons who have the boss's confidence, especially if we ourselves are lower in the organizational hierarchy. As an internal auditor for a nonprofit organization, Ben—a newly hired college graduate—discovered that he needed the support of someone more senior, more experienced, and more knowledgeable (in his case, the organization's accountant) before approaching the outside auditor about questionable reporting practices he had uncovered, and to help him in crafting a solution that worked for all. Perhaps his fresh perspective helped him to see the issue, but he recognized that he needed the insight as well as the credibility of a more senior colleague to make needed changes.[6]

Sometimes we may need to actually choreograph a series of conversations in order to build support and buy-in for our position. In a graduate course on corporate governance at Yale School of Management, a scenario involved an independent director's efforts to influence his board colleagues concerning the CEO succession by doing an analysis of the relative status, influence, and open-mindedness of other board and family members to develop a strategy with the greatest chance of success.[7]

It is also important to consider what kind of conversations are best conducted one-on-one and what kind require a group setting. We discovered in our interviews that often the most effective, mind-changing conversations occurred off-line, in one-on-one conversations that occurred after the initial revelation of the controversial course of action. This is important for several reasons.

First of all, sometimes it is easier and less embarrassing for individuals to change their minds in private. But also, these after-the-fact discussions give the manager who wants to voice his or her values time to do some research and build some scripts. Finally, it is common to feel that if we fail to raise our values-based concerns when the contested position is first mentioned, we have lost the moment. Research has found that this is simply not true: many sources described their success in revisiting decisions that may have appeared definitive.

Still, there are moments for group conversations, particularly if we believe we have or can inspire supporters in the group so our position is not solitary. And there are moments when a decision will have immediate consequences, so the chance to reconvene one-on-one is simply not possible. The key factor is to consider these different contextual and conversational format decisions consciously whenever possible.

## The Critical Importance of Information

It may seem absurdly obvious that we need to do our homework and gather data in order to voice our values effectively. However, it is surprising how often, in our emotionality about a values conflict, we may tend to just blunder in and blurt out an argument without adequate preparation. I think sometimes we do this, paradoxically, precisely because we are so uncomfortable with the situation and want to get it over with quickly. Unfortunately, this response is often less effective—and ultimately maybe even more uncomfortable—than a more carefully prepared response.

This is a phenomenon I observed years ago when I was researching the managerial challenges of building and working with a diverse workforce. Often, due to the emotionality of confronting what appeared to be an unfair or discriminatory situation, managers and employees would just blurt out their responses, in often insensitive and unsupported ways, or they would stifle their responses altogether in an effort to avoid just such an emotional confrontation. It was always surprising to see that individuals who might be quite capable of having intense and even contested debates about the relative merits of a product-line extension or a new organizational policy—with no lasting ill effects on their collegial relationships and while effectively using all the data at their disposal—were so much more likely to forget all their interpersonal and data-based argument-building skills when it came to the charged issues of race, gender, ethnicity, or sexual orientation.

In the stories of individuals who have voiced their values effectively, the importance of taking a deep breath and spending time to gather data is often critical. Managers told of assessing what kinds of arguments had moved their target audience in the past: Was it a well-framed and compelling story about a similar situation? A data-based analysis, complete with spreadsheets, of potential outcomes? A decision-tree or clear and concise graphic representation of the choice at hand? They tried to play to the decision-making preferences and predilections of their audience, presenting their positions in a format that was easiest for them to grasp and hear.

Obviously, the act of gathering data is often a way of collecting allies as well and can provide us with arguments to counter the reasons and rationalizations we are likely to hear for not acting on our values. Perhaps most important of all, the more information we have, the more confident we can be in our position, strengthening our resolve and building courage. Gathering data, of course, requires us to test and retest our initial values position, so that we do not draw false conclusions.

## Questions, Not Answers

Sometimes, both as a means to gather more information and build allies as well as a means to ultimately persuade our target audience, it is most effective to open a discussion with questions rather than arguments and assertions. Instead of giving the impassioned little speech—an approach that while occasionally effective brings many risks—often it is most effective to position oneself as genuinely concerned, posing sincere and real questions that invite the other person to actually name and explain their assumptions. At best, this approach can move the other person to reconsider some viewpoints, as we will see in the story of the diversity consultant in Chapter 6. At a minimum, such an approach can uncover the most critical arguments that we will need to counter.

## The Importance of Understanding the Needs, Fears, and Motivations of the Audience

Often we think that gathering information means an analysis of the pros and cons, the costs and benefits of the situation at hand. However, stories of those who voice their values effectively often reveal an effort to truly understand their audience's personal as well as professional rationale. What is truly at stake for the person or persons we need to persuade? As we will see in Chapter 7, for example, a new employee, Susan, was able to persuade her boss not to alter an unfavorable client portfolio performance report by framing her arguments for honesty in a way that would still protect his position and reputation.[8] Such reframing is not always possible, but even so, an understanding of the audience's true concerns is always useful, if only to avoid building utterly irrelevant arguments or to reveal the need to identify alternate audiences.

## Incremental Steps

Some situations that require us to voice our values are clear and time-defined choices: we choose not to lie to a customer.

However, there are other values conflicts that we encounter where the situation is a more complex and long-standing situation. It is less a matter of a single decision than of reviewing and revising an entire network of relationships and practices. In such situations, we may be faced with mapping out a series of steps that will occur over time.

Felipe Montez, for example, uncovered a set of employee rights and safety concerns that existed historically in an arm's-length subcontracting relationship his firm had with suppliers in Southeast Asia.[9] Trying to unravel and change these relationships from his lower-level position in the company was not a matter of a single decision. In such situations, it can be necessary to work over time to uncover facts, build allies, develop alternatives, and change policy. If a situation has legal implications, it can be important to consult an attorney to be sure of being protected while attempting to make change. Often, the risk may be more organizational than legal, and in these cases it is critical to build trusting relationships and demonstrate organizational commitment in the organization. This type of effort requires a great deal of patience, and it is important to identify and recognize incremental progress as a way of maintaining one's commitment and spirits.

## Framing

One of the most powerful enablers we have identified has been the ability to reframe a position: an opportunity with less than ethical attributes is reframed as a risk we all want to avoid; a disagreement that appears to throw the ethics of our audience into doubt is reframed as a "learning dialogue" wherein we are trying to uncover the true parameters of a possible decision; a win-lose choice is reframed through the use of argument and research as a win-win situation; seemingly self-evident assumptions or "truisms" are reframed as debatable or even patently false.[10] We will discuss this in much more detail in subsequent chapters, but it is important to identify this as one of the most frequently uncovered enablers and approaches to voicing values that we found.

For example, in the stories we gathered from business students at the American University of Sharjah in the United Arab Emirates, one of the most commonly heard reasons for not voicing and acting on their values (that is, one of the most common "disablers") was: "I wanted to act on my values but I did not want to hurt my friends or family." Reframing can be a powerful tool in such situations, so that, for example, we can ask ourselves: "If I don't want to hurt my friends, then wouldn't I assume that they don't want to hurt me either? Perhaps I need to share with them how much this issue means to me, and appeal to their loyalty, too." In other words, this kind of reframing allows us to position ourselves as standing up to the other person precisely because we are, in fact, their friends, owe them our honesty, and expect their reciprocation. Another reframing that can help in responding to this situation is to consider: "If I see myself as a loyal friend and colleague, what about the loyalty I owe to other co-workers (or classmates)? Wouldn't my decision to help you (by cheating on this test or by misrepresenting your mistake in the workplace) be disloyal to them?" What we begin to see through reframing is that equating voicing our values with disloyalty to friends and equating loyalty with not voicing our values needs to be revisited. The loyalty versus integrity challenge is really a false dichotomy once we start to reframe the choices as well as our responses. This is once again a matter of taking time to unpack the emotional first impressions and to practice scripting and delivering a different message.

The need for this time to reflect and practice is another reason why the "tale of two stories" exercise is so useful. In fact, often when managers or business students reflect on an occasion when they did not voice their values, they say something like: "I wish I had done something differently here, and *now* I can imagine what it might have been." This opportunity to revisit decisions and even rewrite the past, crafting a new narrative of "who I am," can be a powerful way to avoid falling into a view of ourselves that reinforces our inability to stand up for our highest values.

Finally, the following chapters on normalizing values conflicts, assertion of purpose, and self-assessment and alignment are all additional examples of enablers that can strengthen our hand when we attempt to voice and enact our values. As noted above, each of the enablers we have discussed can be restated as a disabler if it is absent or if it is poorly enacted.

In addition, there are a number of enablers that are identified as organizational characteristics. That is, they are not directly within the individual's control, except insofar as one might consciously seek out employers that embody these characteristics, or we might work to build these characteristics into the organizations where we work, over time. These organizational enablers include the presence of explicit values and policy statements we can refer to when making values-based arguments. Obviously, the presence of such statements is not a sufficient guard against unethical practice, as Enron famously illustrates, but they can bolster confidence and add one more plank to our platform.

Other organizational enablers include a culture of openness, where dissent and debate are valued, as well as explicit mechanisms for raising questions. These mechanisms can be anything from confidential hotlines and an ethics ombudsman to explicit group discussion practices such as brainstorming exercises and the invitation for employees to play devil's advocate when ideas are being evaluated. In other words, a value for open debate can be fostered in arenas beyond specifically values or ethics discussions. In fact, referring to our decision to voice our values as based in the organization's commitment to open and thorough analysis can strengthen our hand when we do so.

Finally, when an organization has a rich and storied track record and reputation for strong values, many folks have identified this as a factor that both bolstered their confidence and also strengthened their arguments and hand when they set out to voice their values.

All of the above enablers (and disablers) to voicing our values can be called upon or, if absent, sometimes acquired when we decide to do so. And the recognition that we can—and do—choose to speak and act on our values, as well as sometimes choose not to, allows us to see that our failure to do so in some situations does not cast us as unethical for all time, nor does our success at doing so in other situations relieve us from the necessity to continue to challenge ourselves and remain vigilant. It can be dangerous—and in my experience it is always untrue—to define ourselves as either always ethical or always unethical. The first may feed self-justifying bias and the latter may discourage sincere effort. So it becomes important to recognize our capacity for choice as well as change. That is, each situation allows us the opportunity to redefine ourselves.

This is not an easy endeavor, however. As psychologist Jonathan Haidt explains: "We value choice and put ourselves in situations of choice, even though choice often undercuts our happiness."[11] Choice can serve as well as threaten our happiness, simply because it places not only greater opportunities before us but also greater challenges and potential obligations. To maximize the satisfaction and minimize this threat to our equanimity, it is useful to build our comfort and skill around this choice. After all, ignoring it does not mean it is not there. Therefore, identifying the tools and enablers at our disposal and learning to use them can be helpful.

But it is also helpful to recognize that voicing our values can become a muscle or a habit—more of an automatic or default choice. The more we do it, the more we will do it. In interviews, we found that some individuals had exercised that muscle often enough that it became part of their self-definition. Their challenge then became one of strategy and implementation rather than decision making—a challenge that was less emotionally taxing and which leads to our next "way of thinking" about values in the workplace.

## CHAPTER FOUR

# It's Only Normal

NORMALITY: Expect values conflicts so that you
approach them calmly and competently.
Overreaction can limit your choices
unnecessarily.

Even though so many respondents to the Aspen student attitude survey expected to encounter values conflicts in the workplace, and graduate students who have had four or five years of business experience before matriculating appear to have no problem generating examples of such conflicts, our interviews with managers and our observations suggest that often people do not see ethical or moral challenges as a natural or integral part of doing business. We think of ourselves as just working along, minding our own business, when all of a sudden a values conflict inserts itself into the flow of our professional lives. It threatens to derail us. It feels as if it is somehow getting in the way of our "regular" or "real" work. It feels unusual, extraordinary, different. It's an intrusion into the way things ought to be. We often feel or say, "I never expected to encounter this," even when the conflict we are facing is a classic business ethics problem.

Framing the situation as extraordinary in this way can sometimes have a disabling effect. We feel as if we have stepped out of our competent, action-oriented work identities and a more personal part of ourselves is somehow being engaged. This kind of compartmentalization— between our work selves and our personal selves—can mean that even if we typically have no problem articulating a contrarian position on a business decision, we may silence ourselves when it comes to ethical arguments.

Precisely because the ethical conflict is perceived as something separate and apart from business as usual, we are more likely to think in terms of just getting through this challenge so we can get back to business. Framing the challenge as exceptional can mean that we view our actions as not really expressions of who we are. Instead, they are aberrations that we just need to "get past" somehow.

Describing an ethical challenge, one manager interviewed expressed it this way: "In retrospect, this problem really wasn't that overwhelming once I figured out what I wanted to do. But before I had done that, I lied— instinctively I lied—hoping that it just wouldn't happen again. Now I realize such choices are an inevitable part of our business journey and it doesn't seem so huge."[1] Note that this interviewee is not saying that violating his values is normal; rather, he is saying that facing values conflicts is inevitable.

The first time he was confronted with the particular conflict, he was taken off guard and his default position was to lie and try to quickly move on. In retrospect he realized that if he was going to continue in his line of work—as a consultant to facilitate mergers and acquisitions—he was going to encounter this particular challenge repeatedly. That is, he would be asked by someone with whom he had developed a personal as well as professional relationship from one firm to reveal information that would have an impact on that person's career but would also be considered confidential by the other firm the consultant represented. He realized that he had to decide whether he was going to just keep lying—either to his employer firm or to the individuals who requested information—or whether there was a better and more honest way to handle the situation.

By accepting the fact that this was an expected and predictable type of situation in his line of work, he could deescalate the emotion and develop a kind of script that was both honest and also respected his duty of confidentiality to his employer. He would tell such individuals, straight out, that he could not share that information even if he had it, thereby not revealing whether he knew or not. But then he would go on to talk to them about what he had learned from similar situations in the past, how he would think about and prepare himself for any eventuality if he were in the questioner's situation. In this way, he offered the best counsel he could without violating his duty of confidentiality.

The fact is, the script he developed was not "magic" in any way; it was just so clear and unequivocal that it would serve to end the conversation before it got into sticky territory. He could acknowledge his concern for the other person without interpreting that to mean he was required to violate his assessment of his professional obligations, and he could also offer truly helpful insights and advice. In the same way that the other individual was appealing to friendship to request confidential information, he would appeal to their friendship when asking the other to understand his position and his need for discretion. The trick was that he normalized the situation and prepared himself for it, thereby reducing the emotional charge and pressure.

One of the most striking lessons learned from talking to managers who had, in fact, found ways to voice their values is that their approaches and their arguments, although sometimes quite clever, were rarely the types of scripts that any of us could not have thought of ourselves. (Witness the script developed by our consultant above.) What is striking is that these managers believed in the arguments and were comfortable enough with them to actually say them out loud to their intended audience. Too often we fail to express our arguments because we fear they are not bulletproof, but they do not need to be. In fact, the reasons that another person may give us for *not* voicing our values are just as imperfect as our arguments for doing so, if not more. Although the consultant above tried his best to give good advice to his colleague, the fact is that he did not give him the single definitive piece of information that was requested. However, that did not mean that his script was not appropriate and useful. The experience of actually collecting stories of times when folks have voiced their values successfully has taught us that the search for an unassailable argument can be the enemy of success. It becomes more important to normalize the act of expressing our values, and we can do this via practice.

If we approach our business careers with the expectation that we will face values conflicts and have anticipated some of the most common types in our intended industry and functional area, not only can we minimize the disabling effect of surprise, but also we will likely find ourselves framing attempts to speak about these issues in a less alarmist or emotional manner and more as a matter of course. Such an approach can have the effect of normalizing and defusing the topic for ourselves as well as for the individuals with whom we hope to discuss it.

Similarly, it is useful to become familiar, if not comfortable, with the inevitable risks that come with values conflicts. The idea is to normalize the stakes. We all recognize that any business decision—any life decision—comes with the risk that it will not turn out as we hope. Our choices come with no guarantees, and that is also true of our choice to voice and act on our values.

In an interview with Linda Hill in *Harvard Business Review,* Franco Bernabe, CEO of Eni, a major energy-focused industrial group in Italy, comments on the lessons of leadership that guided him through not only a dramatic corporate transformation and turnaround but also a recovery from widespread corruption and public scandal. In particular, he describes the process of normalizing the risks that accompany a choice to respond to values conflicts:

> Leadership requires a willingness to take risks. I took many big risks. But I had two psychological parachutes. First, I was young enough that being fired for pursuing the right ideas wouldn't hurt me—it would be to my credit. I could have worked somewhere else. Second, I never used the paraphernalia of the position. Being the chief executive of a company like Eni, and one of the top managers in the country, you have offered to you a number of perks that can make your life different. I didn't take them. . . . If I had lost my job and gone back to something more subdued and less glamorous—well, it wouldn't have changed my life. So taking risks didn't seem that frightening to me. I didn't have anything to lose.[2]

Bernabe's two "parachutes" bear a bit more examination. The first one—that he could weather being fired because he was young enough to find another job—is particularly interesting because it runs counter to one of the usual reasons given for *not* acting on one's values: Often people say they could not act on their values because they were too young, too junior in the organization, and that they would have to wait until they were in charge to actually make a difference. Bernabe takes this argument and turns it on its head. This is an example of one of the rationalizations for failing to address values conflicts in the workplace, and the kind of reframing that enables us to counter it, that we will address in more depth in subsequent chapters.

Bernabe's second parachute—the idea that he did not allow himself to become attached to the perks of the job—is more familiar. For example, at the end of a Harvard Business School case study, as the protagonist, Donna Dubinsky, considers taking a controversial stand, she recalls some advice a business school professor gave her six years earlier: "He had told students that the first thing to do after graduating was to start pulling together their 'go-to-hell money.' Dubinsky took that to mean that she should never put herself in a situation from which she could not walk away."[3]

By anticipating or *normalizing* the idea that we will have to take risks—even career-threatening ones—in service of our values at some point in our work lives, we expand our vision of what degree of freedom we have in our decision making. The explicit decision to prepare for that eventuality—whether it means saving some amount of go-to-hell money or forgoing certain lifestyle perks or, as we will discuss later, understanding our own particular risk profile—again makes this kind of choice both easier to imagine and more practical to enact. This is not to say that such a choice will never be painless but, rather, that looking at such choices in this way—as normal and survivable—makes them seem possible.

Finally, viewing values conflicts in the workplace as a normal and expected part of our professional lives enables us to more easily understand, identify with, and communicate with those who place us in these challenging situations. If values conflicts are a normal part of our work lives, then those who present these conflicts don't have to be seen as villains. They may well be just like us. Commenting on Roy Baumeister's research on evil, Jonathan Haidt explains: "When taking the perpetrator's perspective, he [Baumeister] found that people who do things we see as evil. . . rarely think they are doing anything wrong. They almost always see themselves as responding to attacks and provocations in ways that are justified. They often think that they themselves are victims."[4]

Although this research focused on human cruelty and aggression rather than the kinds of workplace transgressions we're talking about, it usefully suggests that all people can benefit from recognizing not only their own tendency toward self-justification but also the concomitant tendency to view others as entirely wrong. Diminishing the perceived distance between us and the individual or individuals who present us with a values conflict can make voicing our concerns less daunting, because we can more easily find some common ground.

Perhaps another story can be helpful here. Frank was delighted when he was promoted to controller for the regional sales unit of a leading chemical producer where he had been employed for the last three years.[5] It was a big boost in responsibility and enabled him to participate in the incentive compensation program. As he faced the first end-of-quarter crunch, however, he wondered what he had gotten himself into.

A major customer placed a large order just one week before the end of the quarter, but did not want delivery till the middle of the next quarter. The sales director of Frank's group wanted to recognize the revenue at the time of the order, thereby ensuring the maximum bonus for his group for the quarter. This would mean processing the order, shipping the product to a warehouse, and bearing the carrying costs until shipment to the customer in the following quarter.

Frank felt pressure on all sides. When he sat in the accounting organization, he saw the costs of such revenue recognition problems: the cost of sending messages to all levels of the organization that it was acceptable to game the system; the loss of information and distortions in expectations that jeopardized effective decision making; the cost of records cleanup when the distortion eventually came to light; and so on. He still reported to his old team in the internal control office, and he knew they were counting on him to make the right decisions on this kind of thing. On the other hand, he wanted the sales director and his new unit's general manager to consider him one of the team. He wanted to earn their trust and respect.

This is a classic GVV situation, because Frank is convinced about what he thinks is the right thing to do and his own values are clear even though he himself would benefit financially from a higher quarterly revenues report. Therefore his challenge is not so much to decide what is ethical—he has already done that—but rather to effectively communicate his perspective.

As in the mergers and acquisitions consultant's example above, Frank's problem is nothing new or extraordinary in an organization like his. In an effort to create incentives for the sales force, the firm creates the temptation to distort internal reporting. So right off the bat, he can recognize that as long as he pursues his chosen career path, he will likely encounter such situations. The trick becomes figuring out how to normalize this challenge in a way that reduces the stress and disabling effects of surprise and social pressures, without normalizing the actual abuse itself, because that might create cynicism and reduce his sense of the importance of voicing his values.

One way of normalizing Frank's conflict without normalizing the abuse is to think about the broader nature of his work as controller and the way it can be seen by managers outside his area. Managers sometimes bring conflicting assumptions to the function of internal financial and sales reporting: a simultaneous belief and disbelief in "the numbers." On the one hand, they see themselves as governed by the rules and regulations of financial reporting (both intra- and extra-organizational), unable to act without a version of the numbers to back them up; on the other hand, they see themselves as autonomous agents who manipulate the reporting tools to their own ends. This contradiction is succinctly summed up in the often-heard query: "Can you make the numbers work?" Implicit in this question are the twin assumptions that the numbers can be manipulated and that they are the ultimate arbiter. Sometimes simply naming—and thereby normalizing—this contradiction gives us some common ground from which to begin a conversation about the uses and the integrity of reporting.[6]

Another way to normalize the values conflict— again without normalizing the abuse itself—is to consider what is actually *at stake* for each party in the situation. So for example, Frank might conclude that the stakes for the internal control group and for his company in general include compromised information for decision-making purposes; the costs of cleaning up the data and records if (or when) the actual situation becomes clear; the negative impact on company behavior norms when playing with the numbers becomes the unstated expectation; the actual carrying costs for warehousing the product that was shipped prematurely; and, depending on the nature of the distorted reporting, any potential legal or regulatory sanctions. For Frank and his colleagues in the regional sales unit, the size of their quarterly bonus is at stake. The general manager and the sales director want to maintain their group's performance levels and to save face, since Frank may presume that they have approved this sort of reporting distortion in the past. And for Frank, the stakes include his confidence that he has acted in accordance with his own values; his long-standing reputation with his accounting colleagues; and his new relationship with the sales team.

By identifying the potentially conflicted perspective that managers may have on the function of internal reporting, as well as the varied and sometimes conflicting stakes for all decision makers, Frank can gain insight into how company processes can encourage the reporting distortions he is observing. This reduces his need and tendency to view his new colleagues in the regional sales department as wholly unethical. Their reactions become predictable ("normal"), although not acceptable.

This insight can also point the way to his best methods for arguing against the abuse. In addition to explaining the broader and longer-term organizational costs of the distortion, Frank might explore and agree to pursue systemic changes that might reduce the temptation and pressure to distort reports and better align financial incentives with accurate reporting. We know that there are a number of specific factors that can contribute to the prevalence of fraudulent reporting, such as "a low belief both in the analyzability of information and in the measurability and verifiability of data," and recognizing these factors can provide Frank with a place to start in address-ing them.[7] Finally, although there is no easy way to tell his peers their bonus will be reduced this quarter, he can certainly look for ways to make the longer-term costs and benefits more tangible to them, and he can lead by example since his own compensation is on the line as well. This positions him as "one of us" and gives his argu-ments more credibility.

By taking a step back and viewing his conflict in broad organizational and functional terms, and by identifying what is at stake for all, Frank has shifted an exceptional—for him—and emotional problem, fraught with blame, into a predictable and organizational chal-lenge that draws on his professional expertise in the de-sign and implementation of internal control systems. It is not that the audience he needs to address will necessar-ily be any less opposed to his arguments, but rather that he will be speaking from a position of clarity, substance, and even empathy and he will have positive options to propose rather than only a negative one to impose. His position can move from "thou shalt not" to "let's try"— and whether his audience is persuaded or not, Frank feels as if he has stronger ground to stand upon. This is just part of his job; it's only normal.

Sometimes the impact of normalizing values con-flicts can sneak up on us. In Chapter 1, I shared how de-veloping and teaching a course on diversity enabled me to more naturally, more frequently, and more effectively respond to examples of identity-based bias and insensitivity in my consulting experiences because I was so accustomed to their manifestations and the possible responses to them. Once we recognize these impacts of normalization, we can actually pursue this phenomenon intentionally. The tools for this normalization include recognizing that values conflicts are going to be a regular and predictable experience in the work we have chosen; intentionally putting them into a wider context, reflecting on functional and organizational factors that contribute to or might mitigate the conflict; and explicitly identifying the stakes in the situation for all parties. The goal here is to reduce the emotion and surprise around the conflict itself, as well as to reduce the need to vilify the individuals with whom we may need to disagree. We can understand and normalize their temptations without accepting their actions as appropriate. And we can thereby identify, in advance, the kinds of arguments that will enable us to calmly and effectively respond to the situation and voice our values in the most easily understood and accepted forms.

## CHAPTER FIVE

# What Am I Working For?

PURPOSE: Define your personal and professional
purpose explicitly and broadly before values
conflicts arise: What is the impact you most want
to have in your job, profession, or career?
Similarly, appeal to a sense of purpose in others.

Another way to enhance our ability and likelihood to voice our values in the workplace is related to the way we define our professional or career purpose. If we define our professional purpose explicitly and broadly, it becomes easier to normalize values conflicts as discussed in the previous chapter, seeing them as an expected part of doing business, with costs and benefits that do not seem unusual or especially daunting in comparison with any other business challenge.

If we think of our purpose as moving up in the organization, impressing our bosses, making a good living (or even a great living), for example, then when we face values conflicts in the workplace, we will see our degrees of freedom narrowed by the desire to please those very individuals who may be presenting us with the values conflict. They are the ones who give us performance reviews and raises, or whom we need to cooperate with to accomplish our goals, or to whom we need to make the sale to meet a quota. We may feel we have little choice but to do what they ask.

Of course, the pursuit of any goal—even a narrowly defined goal—can still be guided and disciplined by a set of commitments and rules. Even if we define our purpose narrowly as "closing as many sales as possible," we can still choose to be guided by a set of values and principles that determine how we feel comfortable and justified in doing so, but these "rules" may feel more like constraints we must operate within rather than goals to which we aspire.

If, however, we think of our purpose in a broader sense as building and being part of a company that is a respected corporate citizen—for example, providing valuable products or services to consumers, creating good jobs in a healthy work environment, building a firm that investors can trust to report honestly on its performance—then we will see that we have a broader span of operation when we confront values conflicts. We will have a wider set of positive principles and goals we can refer to and use to guide our behavior. As has been persuasively argued by James Collins and Jerry Porras, "big hairy audacious goals" can be a lot more motivating as well.[1] The attraction of such important and deeply meaningful ob-

jectives—for employees as well as for business students—
is a large part of what has been driving the recent attention to social entrepreneurship across the globe, in both
for-profit and nonprofit organizations, in venture fund-
ing, and in management education offerings (a good reflection of student demand).[2]

Addressing this topic of purpose in a broader sense,
management thinker Charles Handy poses the question,
"What's a business for?" He responds:

> Both sides of the Atlantic would agree that
> there is, first, a clear and important need to
> meet the expectations of a company's theore-
> tical owners: the shareholders. It would, how-
> ever, be more accurate to call most of them
> investors, perhaps even gamblers. . . . Never-
> theless, if management fails to meet their fi-
> nancial hopes, the share price will fall, expos-
> ing the company to unwanted predators and
> making it more difficult to raise new finance.
> But to turn shareholders' needs into a purpose
> is to be guilty of a logical confusion, to mis-
> take a necessary condition for a sufficient
> one. We need to eat to live; food is a necessary
> condition of life. But if we lived mainly to eat,
> making food a sufficient or sole purpose of
> life, we would become gross. The purpose of
> business is not to make a profit, full stop. It is

to make a profit so that the business can do something more or better.[3]

Some may argue that making a profit is a sufficient goal for a business and that values come into play only as the "rules" by which we need to play. This is akin to the "rules as constraints" perspective described above. The point here is not to discredit such an approach— financial success, honestly achieved, is nothing to sneeze at—but rather to suggest that if we define our purpose more broadly, it may become easier to find ways to voice and act on our values when we need to do so. And in an effort to voice and act on our values, we may find it more empowering to appeal to a set of positive goals rather than only to a set of moral constraints: that is, values-based behavior becomes part of a can-do attitude rather than a "thou shalt not" frame of mind. In short, we will see that more things matter to us than simply our next promotion, and that this is possibly true for other people in the workplace as well—not necessarily everyone, but sometimes enough of them to provide necessary support for our position.

Economist Robert Frank has studied behavioral tendencies, and he writes about this effort to bring out the best in our work colleagues in the context of fair trading, stating: "I now believe that the search for a reliable trading partner is not a quest to identify an indiscriminately trustworthy individual, but rather a process of creating conditions that make us more likely to elicit co-operative tendencies in one another."[4] We are not necessarily looking for that individual who will always be fair, but rather trying to create or find conditions that will make it likely that more of us will be so more often. Defining and sharing a professional purpose broad enough to encompass and positively express our values can be one way to create such conditions, because such expressions of purpose can be inspiring and they can signal to others who may share our values that they are not alone.

Management scholar Joel Brockner, also writing about ways to encourage fairness in the workplace, provides examples of ways to create conducive conditions. As Brockner explains, "giving workforces outcome-only directives"—for example, the purpose is to win at any cost—"can be disastrous." Instead, he explains, "by modeling process fairness, senior management does more than communicate organizational values; it also sends a message about 'the art of the possible.' People are more likely to try to tackle difficult challenges when they see others whom they respect doing so."[5] Such managerial behavior concerning process fairness is an example of broadening what was an implicit organizational purpose to include means as well as ends, and then making this broader expression of purpose explicit through named example.

Of course, this example raises the question of what we can do when it is precisely the senior managers who are presenting us with a values conflict. There are more sources of real "respect," however, than merely rank and power. Chapters 6 and 7 talk about some of the tools that might help us tap into them, hopefully engaging the commitment that Brockner describes, even when we are not senior management.

For now, it is important to recognize that this broader definition of purpose does not make values conflicts simple. In fact, it may seem to complicate our lives at times because it requires us to see choices where we may have preferred to simply defer to the "authority" of our superiors in the organization. On the other hand, this broader definition of purpose allows us to dignify our role in the organization at any level. We can see ourselves as part of something valuable and worthy of respect, from entry-level employee to CEO. And it gives us more arguments to draw upon for presenting our point of view.

It also dignifies the values conflicts themselves. These are not seamy little dilemmas that we squirm over quietly and try to forget, rationalizing that they are simply the unfortunate "price we must pay" to survive in a particular firm or industry. Instead, they become opportunities to take a step toward building or preserving an organization that we can be proud of. Instead of normalizing the loss of our values, we can normalize the fact that we will be called upon to preserve them in the face of predictable challenge.

A conversation with a successful investor and partner in a private equity firm provides an illustration of

how revising our sense of purpose and our personal definition of career success can have a profound impact on
our choices, as well as how satisfied we allow ourselves to
be with them. The following is a summary of his story as
he told it.[6]

> In my experience, conversations about
> ethics in business often ring false. . . . It's dif-
> ficult to get to a real level of honesty. . . . There
> is a big distinction between making the coura-
> geous and correct moral decision for one-
> self, and being in a position to implement
> something systemic throughout the organiza-
> tion. And even making the "right" moral deci-
> sion for oneself can often feel like a career lim-
> iting move if the wider organization doesn't
> seem to value that choice . . .
>
> Let me give an example: A number of
> years ago, I built a new area of investments
> that eventually became an over $1 billion por-
> tion of our $2 billion private equity fund. I
> was relatively young for the level of responsi-
> bility I held and I found one of my new peers
> within the firm to be a highly successful, older
> and, in my view, rather cynical partner. This
> partner's approach to colleagues as well as
> competitors was hostile and manipulative,
> and I figured that he would eventually blow
> himself up because of the enemies he made. I

tried to ignore him and stay out of his way, knowing that he probably saw me as a threat since I had made it to the same level at such a young age. I tried to help the guy when I could, thinking maybe I could generate goodwill by being a team player—or at least distinguish my behavior from his.

But I was wrong about everything. Over time, this guy did not blow himself up. He was a talented investor and a good manipulator, and his investment track record allowed him a free behavioral pass from his superiors. What's more, he found ways to push my buttons and to call attention to any possible mistakes I made. He made the environment intolerable for me. I found myself making angry speeches to the CEO in the shower in the mornings, calling for him to rein in this partner. But in the end, I knew that everyone already knew this guy was behaving badly and my complaints about him would not be news. People just accepted the partner's bad behavior because he was talented. And the only way I could change the situation would be to fight at his level, using political tricks or slander to turn folks against him. I just didn't want to go there.

It didn't even feel like a moral or values-based decision; it was just not who I was or the way I wanted to lead my life. Eventually I left the firm and I lost a lot by doing so. Yes, my career has continued to be successful, but not as successful as his in the American definition of the term. I still look back at that experience with discomfort. If I had known what I know now, I would have left sooner because I was angry and miserable for a long time. I just couldn't bring myself to believe that the situation couldn't work out differently. I just found it hard to accept that talented but bad people can, in fact, "win" in such situations. Is that OK? I am still ambivalent about it. I don't think I would have admitted it at the time, but my decision to leave once I knew the situation wouldn't change was delayed somewhat by the high compensation—so I did allow myself to be bought up to a point.

So you may ask: why am I still uncomfortable? Clearly I have continued to be successful in my career. That partner didn't ruin me and what's more, he didn't change me. I was true to myself, even if it took some time, and I didn't hurt anybody else. So what's the problem?

I'd like to say I feel better because I took the high moral ground but in reality, it didn't feel like a choice. It would not have been "me." So the question becomes, why doesn't being the kind of person who behaves fairly and with civility ensure success, given the requisite talent and hard work and commitment? Or, perhaps more to the point here, why doesn't bad behavior ensure failure?

I'd like to be able to embrace the classical definitions of success, accepting that true success is not necessarily about "winning" or financial success or always being recognized and rewarded. I'd like to be able to embrace the idea that true success is more an internal than external phenomenon. But these ideas often seem overwhelmed by real world evidence: they contradict the lessons we learn and the messages we digest every day in school, the media, our communities, about how society measures success. It's difficult for your typical hard-charging, Type A individual to accept that it's OK to make career-limiting decisions in order to maintain one's values.

On the other hand, I look at students and young managers today and am inspired by their instinctive interest in social entrepreneurship, socially responsible investing, and their desire to live balanced lives. It feels kind of schizophrenic: there is clearly a yearning for change by so many individuals, but it is hard to create systemic change at a pace that will actually impact our own careers and lives.

For me, I have begun to think that the

only way to deal with the frustration and ambivalence of these apparently contradictory
messages is to put the idea of success and
achievement into the larger context of meaning in one's entire life. Work success is not
enough; it's just part of a person.

Still, it is important to be honest about
my being able to make this choice. It is easier
for someone who has made a lot of money—
whether it is $5 or $10 million, or $100
million—to make these decisions to redefine
success than it is when you don't have the
same level of security.

So I have begun to take the very challenges that concerned me in my own career
and to work with colleagues who share my
views, to take the very market system we have
studied and mastered in our careers and to
consider ways to use its strengths to support
values-based organizations. The question I am
working on now is: what kinds of changes may
be necessary—at the systemic, organizational,
and personal levels—to support those who
want to succeed in business and still be consistent with their values? And how can I play a
leadership role in supporting those changes?
How can we make the values-based choice
a real, honest, viable alternative for the next
generation of ambitious workers?

This story is compelling for a number of reasons. The partner was working in a highly competitive and unsentimental arena—private equity—and he framed his choices and the reasons for them in similarly competitive and tough-minded terms. He was painfully honest in his self-assessment, noting that he did not always live up to his own values and arguing that even when he did (as when he chose to leave his high-powered position and take a financial hit, rather than be required to behave in a ruthless and dishonest manner to survive organizationally), it felt less like a decision than an instance of just being himself. And he candidly pointed out that his high compensation level was a factor in delaying this decision to leave.

It was important to this individual to present his story in a truthful way. He did not want me to walk away thinking that he was preaching the "just do it" approach to ethical business behavior. On the contrary, he expressed the idea that many business contexts actually encourage and reward unethical behavior, particularly given the way our market and compensation systems are currently structured, rewarding ends over means in many instances.

Reflecting on his story in its entirety, one of the most striking ideas was that for a long time, having done the "right thing" had not been enough for him. This behavior was not necessarily "its own reward," at least for someone who had embraced the prevailing cultural definitions of success that he found in the world of private

equity. And his own subsequent financial success, sub-
stantial by most standards, had not been enough either.
It was the fact that the other guy had *not* suffered—in
fact, his nemesis had done even better than he in financial terms—that had stuck in his craw.

So this story seems important to think about in the
context of considering how our individual definitions of
professional purpose—and career success—can impact
our perceived degrees of freedom and our willingness
and ability to voice our values. On one hand, our protagonist tells a story of how he did in fact enact his values,
but he discredits it by saying it was not a choice. Another
perspective on that decision would be to say that he so
thoroughly embraced and embodied a way of being—a
personal and professional purpose, if you will—that it
made certain behaviors necessary, almost unquestionable for him. That is, even though a part of him fought
the discomfort and tried to find a way to remain and
thrive in his well-compensated position, in the end he
had to leave. Behaving in the way he believed he would
have to behave to survive there was not an option in the
long run, given the identity he held for himself.

Viewed in this way, our protagonist's espoused identity—"your typical hard-charging, Type A individual"—
was in contradiction with his actual enacted identity,
someone who would "make career-limiting decisions in
order to maintain his values." So he felt torn and uncomfortable, even when he acted in accordance with his values. He struggled doubly, on one hand feeling uncom-

fortable that he had not left his organization sooner, and on the other feeling resentful that good behavior did not always trump bad. The task for him was to make his broader purpose explicit, not so much to others as to himself.

This is what he finally began to talk about near the end of the interview, when he says that "the only way to deal with the frustration and ambivalence of these apparently contradictory messages is to put the idea of success and achievement into the larger context of meaning in one's entire life. Work success is not enough; it's just part of a person."

Having begun to define success and purpose in this broader way, and given his own past struggles, he has since committed himself to developing a social venture to seize "the very market system we have studied and mastered in our careers and to consider ways to use its strengths to support values-based organizations." He has found a kind of equilibrium by making his deeper, broader personal and professional purpose explicit, mostly to himself, and by so doing he has tapped into an entrepreneurial energy for this new venture. Instead of surrendering to resentment over the idea that enacting one's values does not necessarily equate to "winning" financially, he decided that what was really important to him was working proactively to better align the two concepts, making it more likely that more individuals would create businesses that are both values-driven and prosperous.

The previous example is about how explicitly recognizing and accepting our professional purpose and definition of success can empower us to come to terms with the potential costs of voicing our values and also to tap into the potential benefits—in renewed energy and unleashed creativity—of that same choice. Because in the end, he *did* make choices: first to postpone living in accordance with his values; second to succumb to his values, to "be me" as he puts it; and finally to embrace explicitly a broader sense of purpose and definition of success that enables him to proactively try to change his sense that the world of business does not always support its best actors.

But what about an example of how a broad and explicit definition of professional purpose can provide us with more degrees of freedom and more tools and arguments for enacting our values when we are acting from *within* our current workplace situation? Various challenges that emerge around internal reporting and accounting can provide an instructive example, because they can arise in so many different contexts and, as we have seen in so many recent scandals and corporate failures, with such great consequences. We will consider some additional examples of this common type of challenge in subsequent chapters, but at this point let us look back to Frank, the internal controller we met in Chapter 4, and then step back a bit to generalize about the different ways we can frame the purposes of this reporting and how this framing affects our ability to voice values-based positions.

Frank was faced with a conflict when the managers and sales team in his regional unit wanted to recognize revenues in the quarter that was just ending for a shipment that was not supposed to be made until the subsequent quarter. This was clearly a violation of reporting policies, and what is more, it would have a number of detrimental impacts on the organization's ability to manage and forecast, as well as contribute to an ever-escalating cycle of reporting distortion. On the other hand, the practice would have immediate positive impacts on his team's compensation and was apparently not a new phenomenon in the organization.

Frank's situation reflects a fundamental conflict between the view that reporting is a tool for managing appearances and the view that it is a tool for managing the substance of a firm's activities.[7] Much of this conflict is due to the fact that the more sophisticated and experienced managers become, the more they recognize that the same "substance" can be represented in many possible ways and that truth is an elusive objective even given the best of intentions. In fact, often "appearances" become "substance" when individuals, such as investors, act on them. In addition, the more experienced they become, the more likely it is that managers will have seen (or been asked to participate in) the "management" or massaging of reporting numbers. This is what happened to Frank when he left the relative cocoon of corporate control and moved into a regional sales office in his firm. The combination of this recognition of how genuinely difficult it can be to define accounting truth plus an exposure to the intentional readjustment of financial reports can lead to cynicism and a surrender to appearances at the expense of substance.

The problem with many appeals to ethics or values in financial reporting as a way to counter this emphasis on managing appearances is that they start and end with a reference to the rules and standards of the function, and miss the question of purpose altogether. Rules and guidelines certainly exist for the legitimate use of accounting tools, but rules are open to interpretation and they can be circumvented if one's motive is strong enough. Knowing the rules of accounting and financial reporting does not mean that we understand the purpose they should be used for. A manager's application of accounting concepts like "materiality" and "conservatism" and "time period," for example, relies on the responsible exercise of judgment, and judgment requires a sense of direction.

Without a clear conception of the purpose for which we want to use the powerful tool of accounting, these concepts become meaningless as guidelines and function only as rationalizations or excuses. This is how we can end up with individuals who attempt to justify fraudulent activity by arguing that it was not "material." And often, in the absence of an explicit wider purpose, managers fall back on an exclusive emphasis on their individual career "success" as their purpose, defined in the terms that our private equity manager used above: "winning," financially. This is what Frank's colleagues in the regional sales office appeared to be doing.

But if accounting and financial reporting are only tools, albeit powerful ones given the impact of the seeming objectivity of quantitative measures, how do we begin to define a purpose for their application that takes us beyond the more narrow conceptions above? First we need to acknowledge that they have a purpose and an impact inside as well as outside the organization. This already positions their purpose more broadly. And then we might suggest that they serve four functions:

> A control function: monitoring activity to assure compliance with goals, rules, laws, and standards;
> A communication function: internal and external reporting;
> A historical function: recording and interpreting the financial history of the organization;
> A decision-making function: creating opportunity and need for dialogue and relationship building around organizational goals and strategy.

The first three of these functions already assume and embody a defined purpose, and we often tend to focus on the control and communication functions when we think about accounting and reporting. It is the decision-making function of accounting, however, that makes our potential power and accountability as managers visible. Viewing accounting and financial reporting as a dialogue and a relationship-building process precludes the narrow application of rules and guidelines as mere rationalizations to support the generation of desired "appearances." Accounting becomes a reciprocal discussion, between different information producers and users, of ends as well as means, and it has real impact on the actual actions of the firm and its managers.

Once this question of ends has been broached, the various possible purposes driving managerial decisions can be revealed and explicitly considered. Frank and his colleagues in control, for example, see their purpose as generating accurate and usable information for monitoring and managing costs and expenditures, as well as making decisions about revenue goal setting, compensation, and planning. But his regional colleagues have different purposes, including maximizing current bonuses and maintaining the sales team reputation.

When such a list is generated, a number of things become apparent. Obviously some of these purposes contradict each other and some of them are more ethically desirable than others. Commitment to some of these purposes depends on the point of view adopted: internal versus external, lower versus higher in the organization, individually motivated versus organizationally motivated, short term versus long term. By naming our purposes in financial reporting, we begin to make the values behind them more transparent and more discussable, allowing Frank, for example, to name the negative implications of a narrowly defined and appearances-driven use of financial reporting.

An explicit examination of purpose does not remove the conflict, but it reframes the discussion from one that focuses on merely managing appearances or appealing to the idea that "everyone is doing it" to one that considers why we report on our sales performance in the first place. Why is it important? What contribution are we making to the effective decision making of the wider firm by doing so? Frank's position is dignified; rather than the "killjoy" or the "naive do-gooder," he positions himself as a savvy manager, someone thinking in organizational terms about the long-term viability of the enterprise as well as his sales team.

Viewing accounting and financial reporting as a decision-making function that creates the opportunity and need for reciprocal dialogue and relationship building makes it possible for managers to conceive of their purpose in broader terms. They can begin thinking of reporting as more than just window dressing—as one MBA student at a top business school termed it—and as serving ends more far reaching than their individual careers. They can begin to name the implications of reporting choices in terms that go well beyond this quarter's earnings report to market analysts, or the impact on an individual salesperson's compensation, as in Frank's situation.

It is not that the choices become easier, but the arguments become much more varied and robust. They come from a place of broader understanding and reflection, rather than of knee-jerk reaction. It is not that all of our knee-jerk reactions are wrong when it comes to ethics; sometimes we have good instincts. It is rather that those types of arguments often seem to be more about us than about the firm, wider impacts, and other employees. By framing our arguments in terms of wider purpose, we offer an invitation that others may choose to accept, to be working for something bigger and better, rather than simply asking them to make us feel better about ourselves.

We will see examples of how individual managers applied these arguments in subsequent pages, but for now, it is important to understand that defining broadly and explicitly naming our managerial and professional purposes gives us a broader platform to stand on when voicing our values. The example discussed here concerns the purpose of internal reporting, but the principle applies in many arenas. The marketing manager in a pharmaceutical firm frames her decision to tone down the rhetoric in a drug advertisement because she defines— and appeals to—her professional purpose as serving the health and well-being of the firm's consumers, rather than more narrowly as maximizing the opening sales of a new drug. The mergers and acquisitions consultant discussed in Chapter 4 defines loyalty to his colleagues as being transparent with them about his obligations and principles, and as offering his best experience-based advice about their career options, as opposed to spilling everything he may know or hear about the impending merger. And so on.

What all of these situations have in common is that by stepping back and reflecting on both our broader personal purpose—why we work—and our broader professional purpose—what impact we want our organization to have—we find a wellspring of new arguments to use in voicing our values, and perhaps even more important, of energy to draw from when we do so.

## CHAPTER SIX

# Playing to My Strengths

## SELF-KNOWLEDGE, SELF-IMAGE,

## AND ALIGNMENT

SELF-KNOWLEDGE, SELF-IMAGE, AND ALIGNMENT:
Generate a "self-story" or personal narrative
about the decision to voice and act on your values
that is consistent with who you already are and
that builds on the strengths and preferences that
you already recognize in yourself. There are many
ways to align your unique strengths and style
with your values. If you view yourself as a
"pragmatist," for example, find a way to see
voicing your values as pragmatic.

One of the most powerful lenses through which to view
values in the workplace—and one of the most powerful
sources of the strength and confidence to act on those
values—is the lens of self-knowledge. A knowledge of
oneself allows the crafting and embracing of a desired
self-image. Managers at all levels in their firms report that

a significant enabler of values-based action is the clarity, commitment, and courage that is born of acting from our true center, finding alignment between who we already are and what we say and do. Some people say they are able to voice and act on their values because they have always had a strong sense of right and wrong and a need to act on this conviction. Psychoanalyst Heinz Kohut describes this kind of moral courage as a person's commitment to "shape the pattern of his life—his thoughts, deeds, and attitudes—in accordance with the design of his nuclear self."[1]

Not all people see themselves this way, however. Let's borrow a taxonomy from Gregory Dees and Peter Crampton's discussion of ethical negotiations.[2] They argue that most people categorize themselves as "idealists" (who attempt to act on their moral ideals no matter what), "pragmatists" (who seek a balance between their material welfare and their moral ideals), or "opportunists" (who are driven exclusively by their own material welfare). Dees and Crampton point out that most people fall into more than one of these categories at different times and depending on the issue, but in our experience with business students and practitioners, the largest group is those who self-identify as pragmatists. They want to act on their values but do not wish to place themselves at a "systematic disadvantage" by doing so. This does not mean that they would never pay a price for voicing and acting on their values, but rather that they believe it may be credibly possible that they could be successful.[3]

This seems a profoundly hopeful observation, because it suggests that there are many who would voice and act on their values if they believed they had a reasonable chance of effectiveness. This observation supports our primary starting assumption for Giving Voice to Values: that most of us want to find ways to voice and act on our values in the workplace and do so effectively. After all, to create and preserve ethical organizational cultures, not everyone has to voice and enact our deepest shared values—just enough of us do.

So if we can derive strength and energy from acting in a way that aligns with our values, it seems we can create that alignment and thereby enhance our willingness and ability to voice and act on our values by finding a way to view ourselves—by developing a "self-story," if you will—that integrates acting on our values with our (already held) sense of who we truly are.[4] If we see ourselves as pragmatists, for example, let's find a way to view voicing our values as pragmatic, as opposed to idealistic or even naive. And let's come up with a life narrative that organizes our past experiences, as well as our current and expected future choices, around a version of our own abilities, preferences, and strengths that can be aligned with voicing and acting on our deepest moral values.

Let's look at an example. We often assume that voicing and acting on our values involves an act of courage. Interestingly, however, some managers report that their ability to voice their values was driven more by fear than courage. Their fear of violating a particular code or incurring some external punishment outweighed the fear of bucking the crowd or refusing their boss's direction.

In one sense, this seems obvious, but it illuminates a relevant debate. There are some companies and business schools that approach their ethics and compliance with a sort of "scared straight" model. They will hire someone who served time for a white-collar offense to lecture on how easy it is to start down that slippery slope and how terrible the consequences are. I have always been skeptical of such efforts, believing it is more effective to tap into people's positive desires to excel (in this case, at implementing their values) than to feed their fears of punishment.

However, listening to an extraordinarily self-reflective and candid woman describe her ability to voice her values as a result of being risk averse and fear driven gave me pause. An analyst for a leading investment bank, she was asked by a close friend to share some proprietary research: "I experienced his request as scary and wrong, but he cajoled, saying, 'It's only me. No one will ever know.' After I refused, he said, 'I've never seen you be that firm with anyone. I guess you've sold your soul to that company.'" Later the analyst commented, "I hate to say 'no' to anyone and I'm basically a non-confrontational person, but I guess I belong to this place for a while and want to be loyal."

This remark about belonging to her employer may

elicit a gasp from readers (it did from the interviewer), who may fear that it sounds as if she is an unquestioning follower who would do anything that was asked. However, the analyst proceeded to share other instances when she had raised questions and voiced her values inside the firm, calling the organization to task when she felt employees were not living up to the espoused company policies and values. These decisions illustrated that for this woman, fear and loyalty actually provided her with the strength to speak up, both inside and outside the organization. Fear and loyalty raised her expectations and her standards for the firm as well as for herself and her colleagues. It seemed that for someone who viewed herself as nonconfrontational, the trick was to frame her values-driven choice in such a way that the confrontation to be avoided was one with the keeper of the values (as opposed to the person who challenged those values).

Other managers interviewed described their decision to voice their values as an expression of their risk-taking and assertive personalities. It appears that one person's fear is another person's courage and that it can be useful to frame the mindsets and predispositions for ethical action as explicitly multiple. If some individuals are convinced that they are fearful, for example, maybe helping them find a way to consciously use that fear to serve a purpose they value would be more effective than preaching courage to them.

In conversations with managers who have acted on their values in the workplace, again and again people describe their ability to voice their values as deriving from some personal identity traits, and many of those traits are not necessarily linked with ethics or morality. Whether it is their personal confidence, their tendency to be contrarian, their risk-averse nature, their risk-taking nature, their need for clarity, or their desire for autonomy and independence, what is interesting is that the trait enabling one individual may be the opposite of what works for another.

Therefore, it becomes important for us to create our own narrative about who we are and how being this particular person enables us to act on our values, as well as what particular risks we face due to this identity. Using the self-assessment in this chapter as well as the lists of enablers and disablers generated from the "tale of two stories" in Chapter 3, we can construct a *personal-professional profile* that is based not only on what is important to us but also on our particular strengths and risk factors when it comes to acting on those values. (See Appendix D for a sample personal-profile survey.) Our familiarity with what we already believe enables and disables voicing our values allows us to name and frame any current challenge in a way that taps into our existing power.

Additionally, we can place a *customized* network of individuals and resources in place to serve our intention to act on our values. Professor Linda Hill of the Harvard Business School uses self-assessment in her leadership curriculum not merely as a tool to identify areas for personal growth but also as a way to clarify where one may need to build in checks and balances. If we know that we tend to defer to authority, for instance, we might seek out a respected contrarian as an adviser on major decisions. This approach is built on the normalizing of personal challenges, just as the discussion in Chapter 4 was built on the normalizing of ethical challenges.

Each of these measures is about making it more likely that we will, in fact, be empowered to act on our values when we confront challenges and that we will be more likely to act skillfully and effectively because we are playing to our strengths and preferences rather than trying to browbeat ourselves into doing something we are not comfortable with or being someone we do not believe we are.

So what are some of the key self-assessment questions to consider when we develop our personal-professional profile? The stories of individuals who have actually voiced their values revealed five areas that, if they are aligned with the way a person frames a conflict, can make it more feasible to voice and act on one's values. These include:

Definition of purpose;
Personal risk profile;
Personal communication style or preferences;
Loyalty profile;
Self-image.

Table 1 offers a list of self-assessment questions in these five areas to consider when constructing a personal-professional profile, such as: What impact do you want to have through your work? Are you a risk taker, or are you risk averse? Do you communicate better in person or in writing? Are you most loyal to your family, colleagues, or employer? Is your self-image idealistic, pragmatic, or opportunistic?

There are really no right or wrong answers to these questions, and individuals who describe the experience of acting on their values will report many different and conflicting self-assessments about why they did so and what made it easier or even necessary for them. Everyone has his or her own self-story, or, at the very least, the capacity to construct one. Again one of the most promising levers for enabling us to voice our values appears to be generating a self-story that allows us to find ways to align what we think is right with who we already think we are. The point here is that how we incorporate values conflicts into our self-story can serve to enable, or disable, our ability to act on our values. It can allow us to play to our strengths, or not. Creating this story is not just about self-knowledge: it is about the way we choose to use that self-knowledge.

This is particularly important in light of research suggesting that most of us tend to be susceptible to self-justifying biases or finding ways to view our decisions as positively motivated, even when we would be critical of someone else who made the same choices. By actively considering our personal-professional profile in advance of conflicts and crafting a self-story that aligns our val-

**Table 1**
**Key Self-Assessment Questions**

---

**Questions of Personal Purpose**
- What are your personal goals?
- Your professional goals?
- What is your personal purpose for your business career?
- What impact do you want to have through your work? On whom?
- How do you define your impact as an auditor, investor, manager, product developer, marketer, senior executive, and so on?
- Whom do you want to know you benefited, and in what ways?
- What do you hope to accomplish?
- What will make your professional life worthwhile?
- How do you want to feel about yourself and your work, both while you are doing it and in the end?

**Questions of Risk**
- What is your risk profile?
- Are you a risk taker, or are you risk averse?
- What are the greatest risks you face in your line of work?
- Are they personal (livelihood, deportation, legal punishment); professional (harms to customers, employees, the firm); or societal (impact on environment, profession, industry, nation)?
- What levels of risk can and can't you live with?

**Questions of Personal Communication Style and Preference**
- Do you deal well with conflict, or are you nonconfrontational? Under what circumstances?
- Do you prefer communicating in person or in writing?
- Do you respond best from the gut and in the moment, or do you need to take time out to reflect and craft your communications?
- Do you assert your position with statements, or do you ask questions in order to communicate and get your points across?

## Questions of Loyalty

- Do you tend to feel the greatest loyalty to family, work colleagues, your employer, or other stakeholders, such as customers?
- How do different conditions and different stakes affect your sense of loyalty?

## Questions of Self-Image

- Generally speaking, do you consider yourself shrewd or naive?
- Do you identify as primarily idealistic, opportunistic, or pragmatic?
- Are you most comfortable in the role of a learner or of a teacher?
- Are you most comfortable in the role of an autonomous, individual contributor or a team member?
- Can you think of circumstances where you have surprised yourself?
- What may have been unique or different about those circumstances, such that they drew out a different side of yourself?

ues, behaviors, and self-image with the kind of person who can make the hard choices and act on their values, we are anticipating those choices and pre-scripting our interpretation *before* we have the chance to be influenced or to rewrite our story under pressure. We make a kind of anticipatory commitment, to head off that tendency to self-justify after the fact. But unlike the typical effort to establish precommitments to values-based action, the commitment here is to being more of who we already are, rather than someone different. The commitment is based on framing our conflicts so that they require the kinds of behaviors and actions with which we are already comfortable and skilled.

Of course, our personal identities are not the only factors contributing to our ability, or inability, to act on what we think is right in times of conflict—or even to remember and know what we think is right. As Robert Frank has noted, the conditions under which we operate influence us powerfully, both in what we believe is possible (e.g., Do we think we have any influence in a particular situation?) and in what we actually come to believe about the rightness or wrongness of a particular choice (e.g., Was our initial values-based reaction misguided?). But, again, taking control of the creation of our own self-story can enable us to anticipate, reframe, and pre-script our response to some of the organizational and social pressures we are likely to encounter.

So let us now turn to some examples of how recognizing and playing to their strengths, as well as reframing their challenges to align with an acceptable self-story, helped two individuals to voice their values.

A number of years ago, a diversity consultant—let's call her Cecilia—was hired by a large U.S. technology development and consulting firm to do a series of interviews with its senior and middle-level managers in an effort to identify opportunities as well as challenges in trying to build a more diverse team.[5] Cecilia describes her interview with a very senior manager, Jim.

It was pretty clear that I was an annoying "interruption" in his day. In a very transaction-oriented environment where time was money, meeting with me was an investment for which he expected little return. He was distracted and adopted a no-nonsense, "I'm going to tell you things you don't want to hear" sort of stance with me. But I plunged into the interview anyway.

I asked Jim some opening questions about his area of responsibility and about the demographics of his large team of managers, salespeople and analysts. When he explained they were predominantly white males, I asked why he thought that was so—and that's when he seemed to finally become engaged in the conversation. He leaned forward and looking directly and intently at me, said: "Let me tell you something, Cecilia. I have tried over the

years to encourage a more diverse workforce
of young managers in my area. And it's really
not fair that the firm starts criticizing us direc-
tors now for not doing enough, because we are
the ones who suffer when these efforts don't
work out. I remember making a real push to
hire and develop a young African American
manager a couple years ago in my department—I was the first one in my area to do
so—but he didn't fare well in the firm. We had
to let him go. And I paid a price for that experience." Jim uttered this last line with real feeling, adding: "So now I just keep my mouth
shut and my head down and try not to say
much about diversity."

Well I must say that I felt a bit useless. Jim's
frustration was exactly the kind of response I
was supposed to identify and help address. And
I knew that although his experience was deeply
felt, there were also many assumptions in his
story that I should point out and hopefully dis-
pel—for example, that one unsuccessful hire
was a reason to ignore all other candidates, or
even that the performance of the hire he described was necessarily fairly assessed.

But I felt frozen. How could I argue with
this very senior manager who sat there absolutely convinced that his story was an airtight
argument against my efforts? After all, he knew

his business better than I could ever hope to and I was acutely aware that, in his eyes, I was just the "diversity lady." I am not a very confrontational person and frankly he intimidated me. I think that at one level, he was trying to. And although I know I am smart enough, my words tend to fly out of my head and I become tongue-tied when I feel I am expected to assume the role of an aggressive and even brash cross-examining attorney. My strength is in dialogue, not argument. I was tempted to just feebly end the interview and withdraw, but I felt I would not only be failing in my professional role, I would be failing to practice my own values around speaking out about diversity in the workplace.

So I paused uncomfortably and wondered how to proceed . . .

Cecilia continues:

After a long moment, I very seriously asked him: "Gee, so what price did you pay, when that guy you hired didn't succeed?" Although in one sense, I was just trying to buy time to figure out how to respond to his arguments, another part of me—the part of my brain that was still functioning—really wanted to know.

And I'll never forget Jim's reaction because it was not at all what I expected. First, he looked startled at what I had said. He sat back in his chair, crossed his arms, and then slowly began to smile ruefully. And he said: "You know, I've told this story many times before, complaining, but no one has ever asked me that question before. They just listen and nod with understanding. And you know in reality, now that I really think about it, I actually didn't pay a price . . . but damned if I didn't truly believe that I had!"

My first reaction at this response was to think "Gotcha!" But then I looked at Jim's face. I saw that rather than trying to mislead me, he genuinely had believed that he was paying a price for his hire. Now upon reflection, he began to recognize that most of the price he had paid was one that he had imagined or just expected. . . or maybe one he had exacted from himself. And this was the first moment in the interview when Jim and I had the opportunity to really connect to constructively think about the way differences played out in that firm.

In this example, Cecilia accidentally found a self-story to tell about her own style and abilities that enabled her to voice her values in a way that felt reasonable and feasible. Rather than continuing to believe that her preference for dialogue and her discomfort with confrontation meant that she would never be able to stand up for her beliefs, she learned to use her open, nonjudgmental, questioning style to make topics discussable that previously had not been—and by so doing to make real differences with her clients. This was a kind of turning point for her, as it enabled her to embrace her preferences and comforts and consciously use them in the service of her values. She learned that being nonconfrontational and somewhat introverted was not a barrier to values-based action; it simply dictated a different approach. Every conflict became an opportunity to learn something, both for her and importantly for the person with whom she disagreed. And rather than that person—Jim, for example—being framed as the adversary or even a villain, he could be seen as a partner in uncovering the truth and a better way of acting.

Or let's take another example. Denise Foley was facing the most difficult professional challenge of her life, and the irony was that its source was the very same man who had changed her career sixteen months earlier—dramatically, forever, and, she had thought then, for the better.[6] After the previous CEO had been fired from the major regional hospital where Foley had worked for several years, a new executive had assumed leadership. After only a month and a half, he plucked Foley from her position as chief of nursing and named her senior vice president and chief operating officer.

Foley embraced her new responsibilities with relish

and commitment. She felt the hospital had given her so much: career opportunities, the chance to complete her MBA, and strong mentors. This was an opportunity not only to grow and face new challenges, but also to give back to the institution. Just over a year into her new role, however, she found herself in the midst of a professional crisis.

After taking a serious look at the situation he had inherited from the previous chief, her new CEO had contracted with a consultant who painted a bleak financial picture for the institution. The consultant advised, and the CEO agreed, that the best course of action would be to sell the hospital to a for-profit institution. This was not an entirely surprising proposal; in fact, it was the path that many nonprofit hospitals were taking to try to solve their financial difficulties. Foley's CEO was entirely behind the strategy.

The problem was, however, that Foley thought the consultant's assessment was incorrect. She didn't know if he was consciously manipulating the numbers or if, seeing hefty fees coming his way, he actually came to believe his own counsel. Meanwhile, the CEO did not have other sources of good information; lacking confidence in the hospital CFO, he had kept him out of the analysis.

The stakes were high for all involved. The CEO needed to solve his institution's financial problems and felt the sale was his best shot. However, he needed unwavering support from his COO to make the strategy work, and Foley had many concerns. She didn't believe the consultant's numbers. Beyond that she was convinced that if the sale went through, the new parent would ultimately close the hospital and sell the assets. She believed this would hurt the consumer: the closing of her institution would leave the community with only one local provider, and price and service suffer when hospitals do not face competition.

Even if she was wrong about the eventual fate of the hospital, Foley was concerned that the hospital service array would be cut: her hospital was the only source of mental health care in the area, for example, but this was traditionally a less profitable offering. And Foley knew that some of her institution's community service and charitable offerings would be cut as well. Based on the local government's past performance, she was not confident that other public funds would be well spent in making up for these losses.

On the other hand, Foley was acutely aware that the CEO was counting on her support. She feared that he would see her challenge as a defection, or a narrowly motivated concern about her own job. He had made a big commitment to her when he promoted her, and she felt a strong sense of loyalty and obligation.

The personal stakes were very high for Foley, too. If she had to leave the hospital, she would need to relocate to find another position, and such a disruption would take a high toll on her family—especially her high-school-age son. And this potential loss to her family was compounded by the thought of losing a highly valued colleague in her CEO. She really wanted to agree with him.

Foley knew that some might say she was being overly scrupulous in her soul searching and needlessly tormenting herself. After all, the CEO was the ultimate arbiter, and perhaps he and his consultant had information that she did not. She was still new to the C-suite, and one could argue that the ink on her MBA was still damp. Did she really have to take on the responsibility for this decision? Couldn't she just do her best to make the CEO's preferred course of action work out?

Foley experienced her decision as very stressful, and she talked it over with her husband at length. She wanted to get a perspective from someone she trusted but who was outside the organization. They decided not to talk to their son because they didn't want him to feel the burden of her decision or to worry unnecessarily. She also looked to a network of past and present colleagues within the hospital as she checked and rechecked her numbers and looked for insight. She remembered the example of an early mentor—an executive nurse—whom Foley had observed on numerous occasions taking difficult stands to uphold her high standards in the face of reports and vocal complaints from her peers. In the end, Foley and her husband concluded that she would not be able to live with herself or continue to take satisfaction in the career she loved if she didn't act on her best judgment.

She decided to put her arguments in writing before she met with the CEO, in order to clarify her thinking and ensure that he could hear her with less emotionality from either of them. Then she took her memo to the

CEO and verbally outlined her position. After presenting why she felt the consultant's assessment was inaccurate, she concluded by explaining that she would not be able to do her job effectively if the sale proceeded because she was confident that her peers and the managers who reported to her would be able to "read" her true thoughts, thereby raising their own doubts.

It was a difficult decision but the CEO decided to look into Foley's analysis. He read her memo and then called the consultant, Foley, and the CFO into a meeting together where they had a frank discussion. It turned out that the CEO was surprised when he really looked deeply at the numbers; he had taken much of he consultant's argument on faith and had not done the kind of close checking that Foley had done. Ultimately, the CEO decided not to sell. He and Foley remained good colleagues and managed to turn the hospital around.

Reflecting on her decision, Foley does not downplay the toll this conflict took on her, but she says she found confidence in her recognition that she was actually *unable* to support a different decision. This belief, that she really had no choice, helped her to deal with the fear that her actions might cause pain for her family or others. She simply didn't believe that following the CEO's original directive was something she could convincingly do.

Another way to express this would be to say that she had a strongly held self-story that portrayed her as someone who could not act contrary to her own best assessment. This story was based both in her moral values but also very importantly in her belief that she was unable to dissemble or to hide her true thoughts and feelings. This story gave her strength, and it probably was part of the reason that others—her husband, her CEO—took her concerns so seriously. They saw her the same way as she saw herself. She framed her decision in a way that was consistent with the way she viewed herself.

But the story does not end there. Foley had the occasion to revisit her self-story in a very interesting way. Shortly after the decision not to sell her hospital, Foley was nominated and selected to participate in a prestigious global leadership development program, which brought together young business leaders for a series of dialogues and educational experiences. She found herself in a room with twenty or so extremely talented young leaders, deeply immersed in a case discussion about what they would do if their own values were in conflict with a decision their employer or their client wanted them to take.

One by one the members of the group coalesced around the conclusion that, under such pressure, they would *not* speak out. Although their apparent candor was impressive, Foley found their position staggering. She was stunned that individuals who, by her assessment, were in such privileged positions with little or no financial pressure—after all, it was only a case discussion—would feel that they had no choice to voice or act on their values. Finally, Foley just blurted out that she thought it would be critical to take a stand.

Foley remembers feeling tense as she voiced her position. She believed that, in some ways, she was already seen as a bit of an "outsider" by the group and she felt that way herself. After all, most of them were highly successful leaders in the private sector. She, on the other hand, was from a nursing background and she worked in a nonprofit hospital; she thought she might seem naive or a bit of a goody two-shoes.

So the question became: Was she naive, or was she bold—even bolder than a group of high-powered executives? In retrospect, she recognized that her decision to speak out to her CEO at the hospital—and her ability to do so effectively—was far from naive. Her financial analysis turned out to be correct and her careful strategy for raising the issue enabled her boss to hear her nondefensively. But when asked why she felt she had no choice but to voice her values while her experienced and highly esteemed companions in a leadership development program felt they had no choice but to silence themselves in the face of values conflicts, she still had to pause.

Was it her status as an "outsider" that allowed her to maintain more perspective, both in the hospital and in the leadership program? Was it her commitment to a larger professional purpose, linked to serving the healthcare needs of her community, that spurred her to look a second and third time at numbers that were driven more by short-term changes in profitability than by long-term institutional sustainability? Was it her good fortune to have strong values-driven mentors and a supportive family that enabled her positions?

Or was it her willingness to embrace her own self-story? Sometimes the hardest part of voicing our values is, ironically, accepting the image of ourselves that such efforts trigger. Of course, this may seem counterintuitive. We may think that the version of our life story we would squirm over is the one where we *fail* to act on our values. After all, isn't that the heart of the so-called *Wall Street Journal* test of ethics: that we should never do anything we would feel uncomfortable seeing on the front page of the *Wall Street Journal* (or the *New York Times,* or telling our parents, or . . . )?

And to a certain degree, the assumption this test is based on is valid. That is, if we consider whether our actions are defensible to the wider public—or if we think of someone whose respect we value and consider how they would react—we will find a helpful reality check on our decision making. It's a way of proactively creating a social context from which we may derive constructive "social proof" for our best instincts.[7] And this is precisely what Foley did when she talked to her husband and respected colleagues at the hospital.

There are a couple of limitations to this test, however. First, people who take actions that violate their values rarely expect to get caught or to have their decision reported in the paper: this is the phenomenon research refers to as our tendency toward "overoptimism."[8] But second, and more to the point here, despite our proactive efforts to create a positive social context and network among family, friends, or trusted colleagues for identifying the right thing to do, we are also still strongly drawn to acceptance from the folks we rely on for our position, or with whom we spend the most time, or to whom we must defend our choice: in Foley's case, her CEO, and in the context of her leadership program, her cohort.

And this acceptance—the perspectives that we hear or assume are prevalent from our professional colleagues—can have a very powerful impact on how we view our own decision to voice our values. Ironically, we may fear that a decision to voice our values—and therefore, not pursue an unethical but tempting course of action—will tag us as "naive" or "unwilling to make the difficult calls" or "not committed to the firm" or "not driven to succeed." Sometimes it is precisely our act of values-based courage that can be labeled negatively by our peers and even raise doubts within ourselves. Even when we have carefully determined what we think the right thing to do may be, we can still find it difficult to act if we don't have *a story to tell about our choices* with which we are comfortable.

Therefore, it can be important to find a way to frame this decision to voice our values—and a story about who we are—that we can feel comfortable with, not only in the *Wall Street Journal* or at home or among our support network, but also in the office and with those with whom we disagree. And in some ways, this self-story is a choice. So what are some useful ways to tell Foley's story as something other than "naive"?

Often people will label a decision naive if they cannot imagine a way to act on it successfully. The fallacy here is the assumption that the limits of one's own imagination are a true reflection of the available choice options. Generating and reflecting on all the times when we or others *have* acted on our values can counter this assumption.

Or, some may label a choice naive because they think the actor has not accepted the "reality" that values-based decision making is an indulgence that cannot coincide with business success. Foley's story illustrates that this assumption is not always true. However, it is not always false either, and therefore it becomes important to consider one's purpose and definition of success.

If we have defined our goals or purpose more narrowly than is optimal, as discussed in Chapter 5— short-term success rather than sustainable success, for example, or career success equated solely with financial success—voicing our values can seem naive or unrealistic. But if we craft a compelling story about our goals that allows for short-term trade-offs to attain or maintain longer-term or deeper values, we may counter, or at least weather, this label more comfortably.

Sometimes the individual who decides to act on his or her values is criticized as unwilling to make the difficult calls, or not committed to the firm, because other employees may see the action as disloyal. They may believe a decision to act on values hurts them or the firm, or it may activate their own guilt that they did not do likewise. Therefore, they try to isolate or punish the person for not participating in the "groupthink" and group action.[9]

One way of responding to such labeling is to craft a story about the choices that is also framed in terms of "loyalty," but loyalty to a different vision of the group (such as to a group that is successful *and* honest), or one that tells of efforts to protect the group from a different set of threats or dangers (a deteriorating corporate culture instead of a slightly lower monthly bonus, for example). It is a way of positing a different group identity that folks can identify with if they choose. The main point here is that we don't need to accept the labels if we do not choose to do so; we can define our own "story."[10]

Foley found a story that worked for her. She chose to embrace a view of herself as unable to act in a way that was out of alignment with her convictions and to use that view to her advantage. Rather than seeing herself as weak, unrealistic, unsophisticated, or not tough enough— all possible ways to frame her responses—she chose to view herself as simply consistent and values-driven.

Some may read the preceding pages and ask: if it is possible to take control of the self-story we craft for our lives, wouldn't it be possible to simply reframe our life narrative so that it justifies any decision we choose to make? And I would respond: yes. But the focus and the intent here is not to persuade folks to act on their values; rather, it is to suggest mechanisms and tools that, *if* we want to voice and enact our values, can help us do so. As Mary Catherine Bateson writes: "In the postmodern environment in which we live, it is easy to say that no version [of our lives] is fixed, no version is completely true. I want to push beyond that awareness and encourage you to think about the *creative responsibility* involved in the fact that there are different ways to tell your stories. It's not that one is true and another is not true. It's a matter of emphasis and context" [emphasis added].[11] If there is a "creative responsibility" in the self-story we create and tell, there can also be a source of creative potential, of empowerment, in that story that can fuel and support our values-based decisions. The invitation here is to use it.

## CHAPTER SEVEN

# Finding My Voice

VOICE: Voice is developed over time and
with practice. Practice voicing your values
using the style of expression with which you are
most skillful and which is most appropriate to
the situation. You are most likely to say those
words that you have pre-scripted and already
heard yourself express, at earlier times in your
career or in practice sessions.

In the Introduction to this book, we talked about a series of essays written by MBA students about a time when their personal values conflicted with what they were explicitly asked—or implicitly expected—to do in the workplace. We noted that even though many of the situations appeared to be quite similar, some students had found ways to voice and act on their values within the organization while others did not. The repertoire of strategies adopted by those who chose to act inside the organization (as opposed to acting outside the organization, by external whistle-blowing or by leaving) fell into some recognizable categories: looking for a win-win solution; changing the boss's mind through persuasion and logic; going over the boss's head within the organization; building coalitions of like-minded employees; and so on. But the pivotal moment was deciding to speak.

We also noted that there are many different ways to speak, and that one of the most valuable approaches to voicing our values lies in recognizing that fact. When we confront an ethical conflict, we often tend to think that our choices are restricted: we can either stand up and declare our opposition to the offending action, or we can remain mute. In fact, however, it is this stark framing of the options that can result in both greater silence and a less effective voice.

Therefore it becomes critically important to understand a few basic points:

- There are many different ways to express our values, and some may work better in certain circumstances with particular audiences than others do.
- We ourselves may be more skillful at, or simply more comfortable with and therefore more likely to use, one approach over another. Thus our ability to frame our challenge in a way that allows us to use that particular preferred approach may be the

> most important factor determining whether
> or not we speak.
>
> - Some organizational contexts or conditions
>   (and some types of leaders) will have a
>   strong impact on our own and others'
>   likelihood of expressing values.
> - There are things we can do to make it more
>   likely that we will voice our values and
>   that we will do so effectively: namely,
>   practice and coaching.

The first observation—that there are many different ways to express our values and that some may work better in certain circumstances than others—suggests that voicing and acting on our values is a learnable skill. As we examine our own experiences and those of others, and as we review research on persuasion, negotiation, and influence, we will see that there are many tools and approaches we might use (such as assertion, questioning, researching and then sharing new data, persuasion, negotiation, leading by example, identifying allies, and so on).

The point here is that just because we are addressing a question of values and ethics does not mean that we need to preach. Often, the very fact that a situation has an ethical component to it leads us to feel that we must gear ourselves up to be saints or even martyrs; in reality, we often just need to be competent and skillful. We can approach the communication challenge with the same analytical and personal capabilities that we would use in any other situation, whether it is a salary negotiation or an effort to persuade our colleagues to use a new software application. And as with other communication challenges, we will want to consider the needs and desires and emotional investments of the individuals we are speaking to, as opposed to focusing exclusively on our own. Reframing "voice" as "dialogue," which includes a goodly dollop of "listening," is another important piece of the recipe. Again, counterproductively, because there are values at stake, sometimes we behave as if listening to the other perspective is in itself a betrayal of our ideals. To the contrary, by listening we sometimes identify the most effective ways to influence our audience.

The second observation—that we ourselves may be more skillful with or simply more likely to choose one approach over another—may seem to contradict the first observation about how certain approaches may work better in certain circumstances. That is, if we have determined that a direct and assertive approach is most likely to work in a particular situation, what do we do if we are personally uncomfortable with or unskilled in that approach? We may need to find a middle ground between our needs and abilities and the needs and preferences of our audience. Even if we are convinced that our personal style will not be the most effective approach in a particular situation, however, we are most likely to speak if we start from the strengths we have (as discussed in the previous chapter), rather than attempting to be an entirely different type of person at a time of stress. Raising the issue, even imperfectly, can still trigger a new sequence of events and conversations.

And often, we may find ways to marry our strengths and comfort areas with the approaches needed, even if they do not seem an immediate match. So, for example, perhaps our understanding of our audience's needs, desires, and perspectives suggests that we should approach him or her one-on-one instead of in a group setting, even if we would prefer the support of our colleagues around us. But we can mitigate our discomfort at flying solo by using the communication style with which we are most skilled and comfortable when we do so. Thus, if our most effective style of communication is storytelling and the use of metaphor, we would likely want to play to our strengths when we set up that one-on-one discussion. Or, if we are uncomfortable with confrontation, like Cecilia the diversity consultant, we may choose to raise our objections through a line of careful questioning rather than assertion. Finally, if we are convinced that we cannot pull off the approach needed to influence our target audience, we may use our own strengths to engage a partner who has the skills and communication preferences required to play that role.

The third observation above—that some organizational contexts or conditions (and some types of leaders) will have a strong impact on our own and others' likelihood of expressing our values—has been widely studied. Much research has been done to examine the impact of organizational systems and policies (incentive systems, communication mechanisms, hierarchy, et cetera) and leadership styles (authoritarian, motivational, open or closed), as well as the impact of group pressures, on our likelihood to speak and act against the prevailing winds in a particular situation.[1]

This research is important for several reasons. First, it identifies the cost of suppressing divergent voices in the workplace: less creativity, missed opportunities, compromised risk management, and so on. It also points out the organizational mechanisms and leadership strategies available to managers and executives who wish to encourage their employees to voice their values in the workplace. In other words, it provides a road map for building organizations that encourage voice. For example, aviation safety procedures are now being borrowed and adapted by hospital surgery teams, in an effort to overcome the kinds of dangerous mistakes that can be made when hierarchy, organizational cultures, or individual self-silencing lead staff members to fail to voice their concerns to their colleagues and supervisors. Some of the strategies that have been used to good effect include formal pre- and post-flight (or surgery) briefings and safety checklists, as well as encouragement of "time-outs" or "safety pauses" that can be called by anyone in the operating room. Such strategies suggest that the normalization, even the encouragement of warning behavior and of consciously stepping back from intense situations may be a helpful way to empower voice in business situations as well.[2]

Perhaps most important, research reveals that often

we are unaware that we have been influenced by our organizational context. We may come to believe that we agree with the prevailing perspective without realizing that we have been influenced and without making a conscious choice. Contrary to the assumptions on which GVV is based, this appears to suggest the idea that we do not have a choice about whether to voice and act on our values. In fact, the power and influence of our context should not be underestimated. Nevertheless, we all know of times when we have seen individuals resist these pressures; we probably can think of some times when we have done so ourselves. In order to do so, however, we need to understand these contextual pressures; we need to be aware that we, our colleagues, and our supervisors may be influenced by them without always recognizing it, and so must remain vigilant and self-aware.

But vigilance is not enough, as Harvard Business School professor Max Bazerman has demonstrated, and too often this admonition is where efforts to encourage values-based leadership start and stop.[3] We also need to understand that resisting these pressures may require strategy and skill as much as moral conviction. For example, as Harvard professor Amy Edmondson explains: "Much research on speaking up has focused on extra-role behaviour, studying when people are willing to speak up about aspects of the organization or work context that go beyond the demands of their jobs. . . . Yet, *how people view their roles* affects what is seen as discretionary behaviour" [emphasis added].[4]

Edmondson's observation that the implicit organizational definition of our role makes some topics "unspeakable" is what lies behind an often heard explanation for why we do not voice our values: "It wasn't my job. It's not my place." And her insight leads us to wonder if we could make an explicit effort to define our roles and job responsibilities in a way that transforms those same, previously "unspeakable" topics into essential items of discussion. This is the proposition that underlies the emphasis in Chapter 5 on defining our career and professional purpose explicitly and broadly. If our role is to serve our customers well, for example, then less than honest advertising practices becomes a relevant topic for discussion, whereas if we define our role as simply producing the ad copy on deadline, we may be less willing to raise such questions about the actual content of that copy.

Additionally, simply saying that some topics do not feel "speakable" begins to change that dynamic. Talking about why it might be so difficult to talk about racial and gender bias in an organization, for example, means we have begun to talk about gender and racial bias. This is a tool—that is, naming and requesting reflection on what can and cannot be talked about—that may be used by individuals at both junior and senior levels in the organization, because it is an invitation to discussion as opposed to a declaration of certainty or a reproach.

In their analysis of "organizational silence," New York University scholars Elizabeth Morrison and Frances

Milliken suggest a number of organizational features that may prevent individuals from speaking up. This research, although discouraging in its finding that it is very difficult to change such a culture, does suggest some mechanisms that the determined individual might employ to find a voice. Morrison and Milliken explain that "the more homogeneous the top management team is with respect to functional training and experience, the more cohesive they are likely to be and the more threatened they might be by the idea of dissent."[5] Although their work is focused on organizational context rather than on individual action, we might infer that an explicit attempt to test our ideas about a particular values conflict with a functionally diverse set of colleagues, and also perhaps to seek support from such a group outside the organization, may help us resist some of the unconscious influence that can lead us to rationalize or even blind ourselves to these same potential transgressions. It may even help us find new ways of expressing our values that would not have occurred to us if we remained more insular in our discussions.

The trick here is to learn from research that demonstrates how difficult it is to buck the organizational system when it comes to speaking up in opposition to prevailing practices or to a supervisor's directive, but at the same time, not to be entirely discouraged by it. The more we understand how we are influenced by our context, the better our ability to use these same organizational pressures to support values-based voice rather than to suppress it. After all, contextual pressures can be used for good or ill. This is another choice, particularly for individuals who have some decision-making influence for setting policy and modeling and establishing norms.

An example of this approach can be seen in the story of Susan, a junior analyst in a financial services company.[6] Her boss, the client portfolio manager, told her to revise her performance report on an individual client's investments by finding a different "blended benchmark" that would make the poor results look better. Susan knew that she did not want to mislead the investor but she also recognized the needs of her boss, who was new to the group and feeling a great deal of organizational pressure due to recent and rapid turnover in their area. The organizational pressures to just go along with unethical behaviors that researchers have identified were all present here: a demand for extreme haste (the presentation was to happen that day); her boss's low personal investment in the client because of his short tenure in the job; Susan's newness to the position as well, which might lead her to feel unsure; explicit and narrow organizational performance metrics (in this case, numbers of clients and size of portfolios under management); the availability of common "rationalizations" for the behavior in question (for example, "any benchmark reflects a set of debatable assumptions anyway so why not change it?"); and so on.

Susan recognized these factors that made it easier for her not to voice her values, and for her boss to behave unethically, but she turned them around and used them to her advantage. She pointed to her own and her boss's newness in the group as an argument for why they should *not* adjust the benchmarks, suggesting that they explain that the poor performance happened before their watch and that they could focus their client presentation on the opportunities they saw to turn things around now. She used the urgency of the request to argue that there was not enough time to redo the analysis. And rather than simply refusing to follow her boss's directions—which would likely have led to his simply assigning the unsavory task to one of her colleagues—Susan made an argument for why she should see the project through because she had a "script" for how to talk honestly but positively to the client.

So rather than being discouraged and resigned in response to research on the difficulties of enacting voice in the face of organizational inhibitors and disincentives, and rather than simply exhorting herself to be vigilant about these pressures (which offers no actionable alternatives in any case), Susan used this research "map" of potential organizational ethical traps as a guide to the very factors she needed to reframe and use to her advantage.

The fourth and final observation about voice—that there are things we can do to make it more likely that we will voice our values and do so effectively (namely, practice and coaching)—is supported by both research and common sense. Research tells us that when leaders talk openly about how they have applied or are learning to apply their values and when they talk about and listen to other viewpoints, they become more approachable and their direct reports feel more able to use their voices in similar ways.[7] We see this illustrated when Larry, a product marketing manager for a consumer electronics firm, asks his market research team to alter its research findings to suggest a greater consumer preference for the new features that Larry knows his demanding and difficult boss, the senior vice president, wants to see.[8] Larry's team members are flummoxed, as they take great pride in the accuracy of their work and they have typically seen Larry as a champion of their care and attention to quality. Because of his past openness about priorities and challenges, the team feels empowered to speak up to Larry and to make the case for presenting the data honestly. Larry, in retrospect, was grateful to his team and took this occasion as a moment to review how well he was dealing with the pressures of his position.

But nice as it is to have corroborating research, we all know this anyway. The more we talk about voicing our values, the more comfortable we become doing so. This is the kernel of truth demonstrated by the World War II "Rescuers" mentioned in the Introduction: those who acted on their values in times of crisis tended to have shared the experience of previewing and prescripting such challenges at earlier points in their lives. This observation reinforces the benefit of actually practicing the process of voicing our values as well as the importance of simply naming our commitment—saying out loud who we are, who we want to be, who we are trying to be.

As we begin to reflect on our own voice, it is encouraging and helpful to recognize that it can be and must be developed. We are not born with a certain degree of freedom or confidence or skill that remains constant throughout our lives. Rather we can enhance or we can diminish our voice by the ways we choose to use or not to use it. In fact, just as we talked in Chapter 6 about consciously crafting a self-story about who we are and who we want to be, we can view the development of our own voice as having a story line or a narrative arc as well.

The power in recognizing this truth is that it allows us to see every experience as part of a learning and building process, even the times when we did not voice our values or when we voiced them incompletely or ineffectively. If we consciously choose to view the development of voice as an ongoing growth process, we allow ourselves room to make mistakes as well as to learn. We do not have to feel defeated or frozen in a less than ethical identity simply because we made some mistakes or missed an opportunity, and we can take even those "failures" as sources for growth and personal learning. Once again, we are taking control of our own choices by reframing them in a constructive way.

Perhaps Lisa Baxter's story can help to illustrate this process of developing a voice.[9] At the time of our conversation, Baxter was a senior vice president for a large con-

sumer products firm. She had spent most of her career in
that industry, working first in sales operations, then distribution, and eventually strategy. Very early in her career, she worked as a junior strategy consultant.

When she was still in her twenties, she faced several
sexual harassment situations. Once, while visiting a client at his site, the company representative told her to
succumb to his advances or her firm would not get the
assignment. Another time, at an off-site team meeting, a
senior partner and vice president pressed his room key
into her hand, telling her he could not concentrate with
her in the meeting and that she must meet him that eve-
ning. The third time, when a senior manager in her firm
tried to pressure her to respond to his advances, she
learned afterward that he was approaching other women
in the firm as well—women who were more junior than
she. Looking back on these situations, Baxter said:

> I never gave in to any of these demands,
> but I also absolutely did not speak clearly or with
> confidence. I was rattled and uncertain; I was
> young and junior in the firm. But I also did not
> experience any negative repercussions for my re-
> fusals. The firm still got the assignment from the
> client who threatened to withhold it; in fact, he
> really wasn't in a position to make that threat
> anyway. And the senior partner I rebuffed just
> acted as if it had never happened.
>
> Each time I successfully held my ground,

I became more sure of myself. You live through a few of these kinds of things and you learn that you can survive. You learn to speak more calmly and confidently when they occur.

Initially, however, I saw it as an individual challenge that I had to handle on my own. It was not until the third time, when I saw that women more junior than myself were also being harassed, that I raised the issue to anyone else in the firm. I figured: how can the organization act to stop this if they don't know that it's happening? I reported the incident to more senior executives in the firm and they asked me back a second time to gather more information. In the end, however, nothing happened—to him or to me.

A number of years later, Baxter recalled a two-day off-site team-building program. After a day of training, the group rode back to the hotel together. When the van stopped at the entrance, one of the senior managers instructed the three women and two of the men to step off, as the rest of the men were going to head off to a strip bar. It was an uncomfortable moment and became even more awkward when one of the men who had been dismissed said he wanted to go along.

At the time, Baxter said nothing. She considered what to do and decided to bring it up a few days later, one on one, with the most senior manager who had been there. She went to his office and said: "You know that experience about the strip bar just felt wrong to me. I've been needing to bring it up with you because it still bothers me. I need to talk to you and to try to understand why it happened and what you think about it."

Baxter was somewhat surprised by the manager's response. He said: "You know, I've felt really uncomfortable about it ever since that night. I didn't know what to say or do then . . . or since. I know now I made the wrong call, but I don't always see that in the moment. Some of this stuff is kind of just the way it's always been. I would be grateful if you would help me stay focused on this kind of thing . . . remind me, tell me the truth."

Although it was not the response she expected, Baxter decided to take him at his word. She gave him feedback on a number of occasions when she thought he had behaved inappropriately, unfairly, or with bias. Looking back, she saw that he took her advice sometimes, but his track record in such areas remained imperfect.

As Baxter progressed in her career, she found herself in the company of more and more senior executives. She recalls a period when her CEO decided to initiate a book discussion group for his senior team. He would assign a recent book and then host a group discussion of its relevance for the firm.

At one point he assigned a popular tell-all book from a different industry, presumably because it might shed light on some universal organizational lessons and because discussing it could serve as a bonding experience for his team. However, the book included a great deal of extremely explicit, rough sexual content, and Baxter felt uncomfortable at the thought of a group discussion with her fellow executives, only three of whom were women. She asked her husband to read it, wondering if she was being too sensitive, but he was even more uncomfortable than she had been. She decided to approach the CEO, one on one, and tell him that she had decided she would not want to participate in a group discussion of the book.

Baxter recalls that she did not pass judgment on the CEO or the book but simply said, "this doesn't work for me." She made no demands and the CEO made no apologies. He did, however, decide not to bring the book forward for a group discussion, and one year later, he remarked that he respected her courage for raising her concerns, adding: "I couldn't have done that if I were in your shoes."

More recently, Baxter faced a challenge to her business judgment that, to her mind, had repercussions for the well-being of the firm and its employees as well as her sense of fair treatment. As senior vice president, she had concluded that she needed to fire one of her senior managers. Before taking this action, however, she had several conversations with her peers in other areas of the firm. She was told that the chairman of the board had a particular interest in this individual and that she would likely hear from him if she made such a move. Baxter was confident in the validity of her decision, however, and did not think it right to protect an individual who could not perform his job, at the expense of the firm and his peers.

Predictably, as soon as she dismissed this individual, she received an irritated call from the chairman of the board, who began to chastise her for the decision and pressure her to reverse it. Baxter waited until he paused and then calmly asked: "May I have the opportunity to explain my thinking on this decision?"

She proceeded to enumerate the things that the individual in question did very well, following with the things that he did not do well at all. She explained that in light of recent decisions about the firm's strategic priorities, *both* lists of abilities would be absolutely critical to the firm's success. And she concluded by asking the chairman if he saw things differently.

Baxter recalled that the chairman, seeing both that Baxter knew and acknowledged this individual's strengths as well as his weaknesses and also that she positioned the decision as an organizational necessity rather than an individual concern, presently backed down and accepted her decision.

In retrospect, Baxter said that the most important factor in this exchange had been that she did not assume the chairman's call was a direct command. Although he was not used to having his opinion challenged, she was willing to ask, sincerely, "Can we discuss this?" And that question made all the difference.

When asked what she had learned about voicing values throughout her career, Baxter identified several "enablers." Some of these are quite consistent with the tool kit we have been developing throughout this text, and it may be useful to enumerate them here in relation to Baxter's story.

## Experience

Living through a few such experiences, knowing that they had happened before and would likely happen again and that she had survived them, increased her confidence and calm resolve. This sounds like the "normalization" process discussed in Chapter 4.

## Positive Reinforcement

For Baxter, positive reinforcement was a matter of interpretation. When she said "no" to the executives who threatened her if she did not accept their advances, she did not experience explicit retaliation. She chose to view this as a positive. When executives and students have discussed Baxter's story, sometimes they argue that the response Baxter received from her managers was not positive, but rather simply the absence of a greater negative. This response is not necessarily inaccurate, but Baxter's interpretation is an example of the power we can derive from choosing to frame a situation in a way that supports our better impulses.

She might have focused on the fact that her decision to report the harassment behavior of a senior executive went unpunished, but instead she stressed the importance, for herself, that she had taken an action that
gave the organization the opportunity to improve and
that supported other women in the firm. She saw her
decision as effective in terms of building her ability and
confidence to exercise her own voice and because it made
certain behaviors visible to the firm's leadership, instead
of seeing it as ineffective because it did not necessarily
result in the outcome she had envisioned.[10] Research
supports this idea that an individual's ability to handle
challenging situations is enhanced by his or her ability to
"make sense" of the situation, to tell a "positive story"
about it, and in particular to answer two questions: "Why
did this happen? What good might I derive from it?"


## Mentors

Baxter watched and learned from other managers and
senior executives who were able to "push back" on their
peers in the firm, thereby demonstrating that resistance
was possible. In particular, she paid attention to the skills
and tactics of those managers who did this "push back"
well. Interestingly, we often think of mentors as people
who have taken a particular and personal interest in us,
and if we do not have such people in our workplace, we

bemoan that lack. In fact, this kind of personal attention has been shown to be invaluable to career success.[11] However, it is possible to take control of our developmental experience at work and learn from the example of other executives even if they are not personally invested in us.

In particular, interviews with individuals who have in fact voiced their values suggest that it is helpful not only to observe and learn from others who speak up about their values, as Baxter did, but also to observe exactly what kind of interventions have been successful in changing the mind of our target audience in the past. That is, when have we seen this person change his or her mind? What was the trigger? Does it seem that certain people have the most influence with our target audience? If so, can we enlist them in our cause? Or if not, can we learn from what has worked with our audience in the past? That is, do they resonate most when someone shares a compelling analogy or story that captures their point? Or are they persuaded by seeing graphs and charts—visual or quantitative representations of the issue at hand? Do they feel most comfortable with decision trees? Or do they seem to respond best to scenarios of positive future possibilities?

The point is that "mentors" can be those individuals who set out to help us, or they can simply be individuals from whom we choose to learn, either by observing their courage and their methods or, in the case of our target audiences, by observing their tendencies and preferences.

## Self-Created Support System
## and Sounding Board

By the time Baxter had risen to become a direct report to the CEO, there was only one other woman at her level. In a few years, there were three others, and these four women decided to have monthly dinners. These get-togethers became a safe place to work out business challenges with a group of people whom she respected, with valid points of view but with whom she did not always agree. They could ask each other: "Am I crazy? How would you bring this issue up?"

## Do Not Assume Opinions or
## Preferences Are Orders

Baxter learned from observation that every expression of opinion or preference from one's boss is not necessarily a direct order, even though many employees, in an effort to please their organizational superiors, may interpret them that way. Baxter concluded that "push back" is important and often (though not always) appreciated. She chose to view her relationship with her bosses as a two-way conversation rather than a one-way interaction, and she felt that this choice was one of the most important enablers for voicing her values. Starting from this place also allowed her to frame her position as an entirely appropriate and even invited response to her boss's position, making it less confrontational, less emotional, and easier for her superiors to change their minds if they were convinced by her. If their initial statements were opinions (rather than orders), changing their position simply reflected reconsideration; Baxter's framing created space for this kind of learning on the part of her boss.

## Form Can Be as Important as Substance

Baxter learned that when she had difficult messages to convey, how she expressed them was a powerful tool. For her, this usually meant calmly, often one on one, and without passing personal judgment. That is, she may have judged the action but she did not presume to understand and judge the personal motivations or thoughts of her boss. She did not waffle on her own perspective, but she claimed it as just that—her *own* perspective—rather than an accusation. "This doesn't work for me. I don't think this is right. Do you see it differently? Help me understand."

As she became more senior in an organization, Baxter also observed: "Leaders have to listen to all concerns, complaints, and even accusations, and learn which ones to give credence to." Therefore, she tried to express her views in ways that would enable them to be heard and taken seriously.

## Know Yourself and Play to Your Strengths

Baxter observed that she had been "raised to follow authority." Such an orientation can serve one well or poorly, depending on the ability, intelligence, and integrity of the "authority" one follows. Stories abound of individuals who were "just following orders," and who therefore took actions that they personally considered unethical.[12]

Baxter, however, appeared to have found ways to use her self-identified tendency to follow authority in order to increase her effectiveness at voicing her values. She found a way to reframe her own tendencies so that they became enablers for values-based action. Baxter had a kind of default position of respect toward authority, but rather than letting this respect silence her, she used it to design careful and even deferential ways to question that authority. As she noted above, instead of forcing herself to voice her discomfort with certain practices in the moment, confrontationally and publicly, she tended to take time to reflect, to determine a way to express those views that were a true priority to her, but in a way that invited the other person to consider her viewpoint seriously and nondefensively. She *owned* her own views, in a way that was still respectful of the other person's formal authority. Her bosses knew that she raised an issue only when it was important and that her commitment to the organization was unquestionable.

Although there may be some disadvantages to Baxter's methods (for example, the "behind closed doors" approach can provide the opportunity to sweep issues under the rug, as may have happened with her efforts to address harassment behavior in her early career), there are also advantages. But most important, it was a style with which Baxter was quite skilled. She played to her strengths: her ability to clearly and nondefensively express her own views, and to honestly ask for and hear others' viewpoints. Another person might take an entirely different approach and be just as effective.

Finally, although Baxter respected authority, she also knew and respected herself. She understood that there were some cases where she just needed to draw the line, and she did. Although her communication style may have been sensitive and nonconfrontational, the content was clear when it needed to be. She said no, clearly and immediately, to unwanted advances; she removed herself from a discussion that felt inappropriate; and she acted on and defended her own business judgment when it came to employment decisions.

### Frame Choices in Ways That Align Them with Broad, Widely Shared Purpose

As discussed in Chapter 5, it is possible for an individual who sees herself as respecting and following authority to be quite firm when she frames her choices as "in line with" the higher organizational good. For example, Baxter went public about her sexual harassment—as opposed to simply dealing with it personally—when she realized that it was affecting others in the organization and concluded that the firm could not take action if they did not know about it. And she fired an executive, against the wishes of the board chairman, when she was firmly convinced that it would hurt the firm if she did not do so—and that became her most powerful argument for explaining and defending her action.

## Practice

As she progressed in her career, Baxter became more polished, more confident, and more skillful at voicing her values. But she felt that it was the experience and the practice in expressing them, even clumsily, that built this muscle, and not simply the fact that she was more senior in the firm. This idea—that practice is powerful—is one of the foundational ideas in this book, of course.

Lisa Baxter's story illustrates how we can develop and strengthen the ability to voice our values over a career, through experience, reflection, learning, and practice. As we have seen, creating a self-story to assess, interpret, and build upon our experiences with voicing values is a powerful way to reframe our failures or our mistakes and to multiply our successes. Rather than viewing her early inability to move her organization to deal with sexual harassment as a story of failure, for example, she chose to recognize it as a building block in a different story, that of her own development as a values-driven executive.

But there is another narrative arc or story line that is critical to understand if we are to voice and act on our values in our careers. In conversations and interviews with countless managers and business students, one of the most commonly heard refrains is "I wish I could have voiced and acted on my values, but I am too junior in the organization . . . or too senior . . . or I'm stuck in the middle . . ."

Often people feel they are unable to address values conflicts when they are at lower levels in an organization because they do not have the power, the influence, the access, or even the necessary information and perspective. They may think they know what is right but lack the credibility or leverage to get it done. Or they may begin to question their own perspectives, asking themselves, "Who am I to question the whole organization, or my more experienced supervisor, or even presumed industry practice?"

On the other hand, once they reach higher levels, or even the top of an organization, they will feel the increased burden of others' livelihoods and well-being; they will have increased personal stakes themselves (position, wealth, the esteem of others); and they will more clearly see the complexity of taking corrective actions. And of course, if they have suppressed their values conflicts until this point, they themselves and their values may no longer be what they once believed they were.

They may be engaged in a kind of willed blindness, either unconsciously or consciously.

And then when we speak to those who are neither very junior nor very senior in an organization, they will complain that they are squeezed between the two positions, neither junior enough nor senior enough to take the risks they deem necessary to voice their values.

So the challenge is that it may never appear to be the "right time" to take on such values conflicts. Of course, the flip side of this is that it may never be the "wrong time" either. And despite the persuasive arguments for why it is difficult to voice one's values at each level in an organization, we have also found individuals who have, in fact, done so successfully at every level of their organization, and it can be helpful to learn from these examples. Admittedly there are situational barriers at each level, but there are also situational enablers. Although the different degrees of freedom that senior executives experience, compared with middle- or lower-level employees, may require that problems be framed differently, we have seen that action is not necessarily precluded simply due to position.

One of the useful reframings we have found for finding ways to act, regardless of one's level in an organization, is to focus on the barriers to action that someone at a *different* level might face. The flip side of these barriers is often an enabler at one's own level. So for example, a senior person in an organization can ask what might discourage a more junior manager from values-based action in a particular situation. Typically these level-based arguments are implicitly or explicitly based on an assumption that the specific barriers are not present at a different level in the organization. This question can then be followed by asking what tactics and avenues might be used for voicing values by a senior manager that may not be available to a more junior manager.

By framing the question in this way, we position ourselves as trying to solve the problem of how to take a stand, rather than whether to do so. In addition, it becomes possible to start from the assumption that, despite the greater complexities, the more senior executive also has greater tools at his or her disposal. However, a senior manager may not learn of certain practices until they have already reached a dangerous scale, so the consequences of any action could be greater.

Individuals at lower levels in the organization, on the other hand, may be in a position to effect small decisions that, if left unaddressed, could eventually snowball, resulting in greater consequences for the company and for the individual. If they use the same technique— asking what the barriers to action might be at a different level than their own (in this case, a more senior level)— they also may begin to identify the enablers and the degrees of freedom for the junior employee that are implicit in the barriers identified for senior executives.

The point is, we have another choice about how we construct our career narrative. We are capable of creating a story line for our careers that focuses on the barriers at each level. Or recognizing that, viewed in that way, there will never be a "right time" to act, but we can alternatively choose to create a career narrative that focuses on what we *can* do, given our level and position. In this way, we can marry idealism with pragmatism.

Some examples of this kind of career narrative emerged in interviews with managers. Two individuals, one very senior and one very junior, were responsible for managerial control in their organizations, and both encountered values conflicts concerning honest and accurate reporting. Jeff Salett was about to assume a promotion to corporate controller in a major industrial products firm when he was advised by colleagues to adjust financial restructuring charges to present a more positive financial picture of the firm's performance. And then there was Ben, with an undergraduate degree in accounting, newly hired to manage internal and external reporting for a small nonprofit organization, who noticed that reports for in-kind gifts were being overstated by the donors for tax write-off purposes and that his organization was a passive accomplice in this activity.[13]

The organizations were different; the scale and stakes of the activity were different; and obviously, the level and clout of the individuals—Jeff and Ben—were also very different. However, they both found ways to proceed that drew upon their own degrees of freedom and resources. Jeff decided to seize the inherent advantage of the moment—that is, the fact that he was about to assume his promotion to a very senior role—and to make that his source of strength. He realized that if reporting distortions was his first act as corporate controller, he would be essentially surrendering the credibility and opportunity that comes with this role. He knew that his imminent entry into this job could also be framed as a reason not to act ("Don't alienate the allies you will need in the firm before you even start"), but he believed this line of thinking would be a trap and that it would never get easier.

Salett went directly to the CEO and explained the situation and his decision not to adjust the numbers. He also told the CEO that upon assuming the role of corporate controller, he planned to announce a new guiding vision for the control function of the company based on an explicit commitment to integrity. He planned to communicate this message to the outside auditors, as well as to the approximately two hundred control professionals, and asked for the CEO's support in communicating the message to the top one hundred and fifty executives.

He did not ask permission; he simply informed the CEO of his intentions, respectfully but firmly. He began from the assumption that the CEO would share his commitment to integrity and framed his comments as if that were true; he approached the CEO as if they were, "of course, on the same side." He explained that he assumed that the CEO would rather know in advance about the situation and how he intended to deal with it. He used examples of other firms' experiences and he defined success as long-term survival and maintenance of an impeccable reputation for integrity. The CEO gave him his full support. Salett concluded that if you have the power of position, you have a platform that allows you to drive change.

Often when very senior executives talk about the things that "disable" them from voicing their values, they talk about risk—their own, the firm's, the employees', and so on. With regard to company risk and employee risk, Salett was convinced that it would be greater if he did not act on his values. And the degree of personal risk he was taking depended on how willing he was to settle for the status quo. He knew that if he could not make the changes he envisioned, there would be far greater issues down the line and he would not want to stay at the company. Salett's "risk calculus" had a longer time frame than that of some of his colleagues. Therefore, the only risk for him was in not trying to make change, suggesting that "risk" is in the eye of the beholder. In fact, Salett commented, "people's willingness to voice their values depends on how happy they are living under bad conditions." In his case, he was not happy with the way he had come to realize the company was operating.

But what about Ben, who did not have the power of the position that Salett held? As it turns out, Ben decided to use his junior status to his advantage. He approached the nonprofit's executive director and its accountant with an open, inquisitive stance. He assumed the role of a seemingly naive questioner rather than an accuser. It turned out that the executive director did already know of the problem but was overwhelmed by more than this issue.

She did not take action and shortly after, she left the organization. Ben concluded that her decision to leave was already in the works when he approached her and his questions were not a priority for her.

On the other hand, the accountant was willing to accompany Ben to the external auditor, and together they came up with a resolution. They developed an "average cost per box" and they informed donors that they would assign that value to their donations unless they submitted a written audit of the (perhaps greater) value for the IRS. They were transparent with the IRS about their approach. Donors, although perhaps not thrilled with the new method, did not see it as a personal accusation.

Reflecting on what allowed him to speak up, Ben identifies several factors.

- "Fear enabled me." He wanted to protect himself and the organization from the IRS.
- "Ego enabled me." He was an ambitious, confident kid. He had already been positively rewarded for speaking up, questioning a different accounting issue in his job interview.
- "My desire to learn and understand enabled me." He liked to ask questions and to think through problems for himself.

And interestingly, none of these factors were curtailed by his lower status in the organization; in fact, one could argue that it was easier to act in this way because he was new and junior.

The point here is not to argue that Jeff's and Ben's solutions would work in every situation. Rather, they found ways to play to the strengths of their relative organizational levels and to develop a tone of "voice" that suited those levels. Doing this involved crafting a story line about their positions that focused on the advantages rather than the disadvantages of whatever role they held.

In this discussion of voice, we have identified ways to build our ability and our likelihood to express our values. We have identified organizational factors that can inhibit this likelihood, and in Susan's story we have offered ways that individuals might reframe those factors so that they can allow or even encourage voice. Lisa Baxter's story has shown how a voice is developed over the course of a career through practice and experience. Jeff and Ben demonstrated how one's level in an organization can be a source of both challenge and also opportunity in attempting to find the best tone of voice for expressing our values.

Implicit in all of this discussion is the idea that the more we practice using our voice when it comes to values, the more skillful, confident, and comfortable we can be in doing so. This is not to say that if we failed to do so in the past, we cannot start to do so now. In fact, as we have said, every one of us has both voiced our values and also failed to do so at some points in our lives. Rather it is important to tell a story to ourselves that positions both the failures and the successes as part of a process in building a voice. And the practice we need to voice our values can occur both in medias res—that is, in our professional lives themselves—and also in intentionally choreographed "rehearsals" that we set up with peers.

But now that we have considered how to think about ourselves and our organizations, and how to build our confidence and self-story as individuals who want to voice their values, what are some ways to develop the actual scripts for what we might say? We will consider this subject in Chapter 8.

## CHAPTER EIGHT

# Reasons and Rationalizations

REASONS AND RATIONALIZATIONS: Anticipate
the typical rationalizations given for
ethically questionable behavior and identify
counterarguments. These rationalizations are
predictable and vulnerable to reasoned response.

When we encounter values conflicts in the workplace, they typically come with a set of reasons and rationalizations that are offered to justify pursuing a particular course of action. These are the objections we hear from our colleagues when we try to point out an ethical problem in the way things are being done. Sometimes we don't even hear them; we simply anticipate them because they are the unspoken assumptions—the seeming truisms—of the organization. And they can confound our best attempts to fulfill our own sense of organizational and personal purpose.

It is extremely difficult to make a strong argument against the prevailing winds if we feel we are in the minority, or if we don't feel we have the time to come up with a workable alternative, or if we don't want to take a chance in presenting a half-baked response. So this chapter is about taking sufficient time to come up with a fully baked and pretested response to some of the most common challenges we are likely to face in our workplaces. Spending time with others who are reading and discussing this chapter (a "majority" for the moment) can help in learning to unpack and reason through the most common and intractable arguments against ethical and responsible management, and to practice generating responses to these common arguments.

Jonathan Haidt's research tells us that our actions are often directed by our emotions and instincts more than reason, but that achieving peace of mind requires us to develop a way of making sense of these actions, even if it's after the fact.[1] This seems consistent with the tendency to act in ways that seem most comfortable or safe in our particular organizational context, even when those tendencies conflict with our sense of right and wrong. This observation might seem to militate against the value or usefulness of developing cognitive or rational arguments for acting on our values in advance of the actual situation. That is, what's the point of coming up with a good argument if people are going to follow their emotions and go with the herd anyway?

In fact, this research may be a good explanation for some of the limitations of academic business ethics education and corporate ethics training. If the purpose of these discussions is to persuade people to behave ethically even when their emotions are pushing them in a different direction, then we are engaged in a steep uphill battle. If, on the other hand, the real purpose of the conversation is to prepare folks to be able to do what they already want to do—although they fear it could be too difficult to do so—then we are working with rather than against the emotional grain, and reframing our objective in this way allows us to appeal to the more positive and implementation-oriented predilections of our audience.

Let's just consider what Haidt's observation would mean if we accepted the starting assumption that the majority of us would like to act on our values, as long as we could do so without feeling like we were putting ourselves at a systematic disadvantage (that is, as long as we thought there might be a reasonable chance to be effective or to succeed).[2] And let's ask whether it is possible that the emotions that lead us to want to act on our values and to want to see ourselves as the kind of individuals who do so could become just as strong as, or even stronger than, those that lead us to default to organizational pressures? Doesn't it then seem possible that we might even strengthen these emotions if we could practice developing and delivering persuasive scripts for voicing our values *before* the fact, thereby making the option of doing so feel more real? We might feel less defeated by the context if only we thought we had a persuasive leg to stand upon. Every one of us can think of times when we felt a nagging doubt or discomfort about the way our team, our employer, or even our group of friends was behaving, but we felt silenced by the inability to think of a persuasive argument, in the moment, to use to resist the trend. We may even have begun to question our own instincts and initial judgment because we could not find a viable way to respond to the reasons and rationalizations around us.

So here we are going to take that time to identify and analyze the most frequently heard reasons and rationalizations for unethical behaviors, and develop persuasive arguments that we might use to respond to them. These arguments are not intended to persuade ourselves to behave ethically if we don't want to; rather, they are intended as arguments we can use to effectively express the views and preferences we already hold. This pre-scripting is both a cognitive exercise as well as a behavioral and emotional one. We examine and create substantive responses to commonly heard rationalizations, but we also take time to practice expressing them, at least in writing but preferably out loud to colleagues, friends, and peers who stand in as proxies for the very folks we would need to persuade in the workplace.

In order to develop effective scripts, we will want to consider the values conflict at hand carefully and answer the following questions:

- What is the action or decision that we believe is right?

- What are the main arguments against this course that we're likely to encounter? What are the reasons and rationalizations we will need to address?
- What's at stake for the key parties, including those who disagree with us? And what's at stake for us?
- What are our most powerful and persuasive responses to the reasons and rationalizations we need to address? To whom should the argu-ment be made? When and in what context?

Interestingly, these questions are not asking us to apply ethical analysis. Rather they are all about understanding the reasons and motivations—both rational and emotional, organizational and personal, ethical and perhaps unethical—that guide the behavior and choices of those with whom we want to communicate and, by extension, of ourselves.

What can make this approach particularly useful for tackling values-based conflicts is that, after a while, we will begin to recognize familiar categories of argument or reasons that we typically hear from someone defending an ethically questionable behavior. And, similarly, there are some useful questions, persuasive arguments, and ways of framing our own role or purpose, and that of our organization, which can help us respond persuasively to these frequent arguments.

Finally, the very act of recognizing and naming the argument can reduce its power because it is no longer unconscious or assumed; we have made it discussable and even put it into play with equal or stronger counter-arguments. Choice becomes possible, and that is what this process is all about. Beyond that, the choice to voice our values can become a habit, more of a default position, with less emotional baggage attached to it. We can respond calmly because our responses are second nature and don't require the frantic mental and emotional flailing about to access them that they often do without this kind of pre-scripting and rehearsal.

Let's take time here to identify some of the familiar categories of values conflict and of rationalization, as well as some possible types of response, by way of illustration. First, there are a number of different ways to categorize the types of values-based conflicts we encounter as well as the typical arguments we might hear to support them. For example, values-based conflicts might be classified by the generic type of dilemma, by the function or industry where we would most likely encounter them, or by the type of argument or rationalization we might face when responding to them. Sometimes these categorization schemes may overlap. Nevertheless, they suggest different ways of enhancing our ability to recognize and respond to values-based conflicts.

So if we want to categorize values conflicts by generic type of dilemma, one such categorization is described by Rushworth Kidder and based on research at the Institute for Global Ethics. Kidder suggests that despite their myriad manifestations, most ethical dilemmas fall into four categories or patterns:

Truth versus loyalty
Individual versus community
Short term versus long term
Justice versus mercy[3]

Kidder is talking here about conflicting values, not values versus a lack of values. This is the classic "right versus right" dilemma, as opposed to a "right versus wrong" choice. Do we focus on the needs and wants of the individual or the needs and wants of the community, for example? Or do we define our organizational policies with an emphasis on clear and consistent justice in response to violations, or with an eye to mercy and second chances? And of course, it is true that many times we *do* face situations where our own values are indeed conflicted. On the other hand, sometimes a values conflict only appears to be a true right-versus-right dilemma because of the way the choices are framed. In other words, framing a choice as a dilemma between two "rights" can itself sometimes be a form of rationalization, obscuring the "wrong" that may lurk there. Thus, being prepared to recognize the ways that the framing of a choice may call different values into play can be useful and put us on guard against this form of misrepresentation.

Let's look at an example of this. A colleague on our

company sales team may use an appeal to personal loyalty as a way to persuade us to violate our commitment to integrity when he or she asks us to keep silent about deceptive sales tactics. Our colleague has presented his or her appeal as a classic right-versus-right dilemma, "truth versus loyalty." But now that we are prepared to recognize the familiar pattern in this values conflict, we can also recognize when it is being used as a rationalization and begin to generate an effective response. The conflict moves from the particular and the immediate moment— wanting to help or protect a friend—into a broader, more general context, and we begin to see it more clearly at this distance. Once we recognize that attempts to persuade us to violate our own values are often framed in this way, we might recognize that our colleague is not showing the same loyalty *to* us (by not respecting our personal integrity) that he or she is asking *from* us. That is, loyalty does not mean doing anything our friend would prefer, but rather it is an appeal to what our friend can *legitimately* ask or expect from us, and us from him or her. This is not to say that genuine "truth versus loyalty" dilemmas do not exist, but seeing it this way helps us recognize when this familiar pattern is being used to mask a less legitimate choice.[4]

The point here is that becoming familiar with these common categories of values conflicts can help us to recognize when they lie beneath the challenge we face, but also to recognize when the challenge is only framed as a right-versus-right type of dilemma. We can more easily assess and, if necessary, see through this kind of appeal because we have named the values at issue—loyalty, truth, mercy, justice, et cetera—and therefore can more clearly consider whether it is actually in play.

Another scheme by which we might categorize values conflicts is according to the particular functional area or industry where they typically arise. For example, there are some challenges more common in the world of operations managers than in the world of financial managers or sales professionals. Familiarizing ourselves with the types of challenge most prevalent in our own work, as well as the common pressures, incentives, and disincentives that affect our choices, can help prepare us for both normalizing and effectively responding to these challenges. This was the lesson we learned in Chapter 4 from the consultant who realized that as long as he worked in the area of mergers and acquisitions, he was likely to confront situations where individual colleagues and companies would place conflicting demands on him regarding the protection and sharing of confidential information. Once he recognized this, he developed a kind of script that reflected his values, and in this way he would no longer be caught off guard and default to lying.

Once we identify the common challenges in our particular line of work, it is especially useful to look for and note any examples of individuals who have effectively voiced and acted on their values in this type of situation. These will not always be easy to find, but even one story can be powerful, as it demonstrates that there can indeed be options. In fact, this was one of the initial drivers behind the development of the Giving Voice to Values curriculum collection: to collect and share positive examples of individuals who effectively enacted their values. These examples can also be mined for actual arguments and tactics that have worked in the past, and they can provide encouragement not only for ourselves but for the individuals we are trying to influence.

Finally, we might consider the most frequent categories of argument or rationalization that we face when we speak out against unethical practice. Some of the most common arguments include:

Expected or Standard Practice: "Everyone
    does this, so it's really standard practice.
    It's even expected."
Materiality: "The impact of this action is not
    material. It doesn't really hurt anyone."
Locus of Responsibility: "This is not my respon-
    sibility; I'm just following orders here."
Locus of Loyalty: "I know this isn't quite fair
    to the customer but I don't want to hurt
    my reports/team/boss/company."

As we begin to recognize these categories of argument, we will become more adept at drawing upon responses to each of them. For example, the appeal to expected or standard practice is often an exaggeration. If everyone actually were doing "it" (whatever "it" is), what would be the consequences for business practice and customer trust? And if the practice is really accepted, why are there so often laws, rules, or policies against it? Would we be comfortable if everyone knew we were doing this? Whom wouldn't we want to know, and what does that tell us? This is where those stories of positive behavior that we talked about collecting can be very helpful, as they demonstrate that "everyone" is not, in fact, doing it.

With regard to the materiality argument, it becomes important to recognize that casting the question in terms of materiality, to begin with, shifts responsibility for decisions away from the manager and onto a set of external guidelines. But those guidelines for determinations of materiality are often ambiguous. Rather than being objective, they can depend on the method of measurement being employed. Additionally, some practices are considered fraudulent, regardless of their relative size; that is, some things can't be just a little wrong. Each of these recognitions can be the seed from which our response to the rationalization can be built.

The question of responsibility is another well-considered topic in ethics literature, and numerous guidelines have been developed for assessing whether or not we are ethically responsible for or required to act in a particular situation. For example, in a discussion of "social injury" that we have not caused ourselves, several ethicists have coined the "Kew Gardens Principles" (from the Kitty Genovese tragedy) to determine our level of responsibility for intervention. These principles are: need (that is, a critical need exists, and the greater the need, the greater the obligation); proximity (meaning not only nearness to the negative action or situation but also awareness of it, as a person is not responsible for something he or she couldn't know about); capability (that is, the ability to act to counter or resist the wrong); and last resort (responsibility to act increases if there are few or no others who could do so).[5]

Although such checklists or tests are usually developed by ethicists to help individuals decide whether they are obligated to act in a particular situation, our purpose here is different. We are beginning from the position that we want to act—we have already concluded we are indeed responsible for voicing our values—and therefore we are trying to answer the question: "How can we do so most effectively?" So in this context, this checklist can be helpful as the source of arguments that we might use in our efforts to persuade others in the company to share this responsibility: for example, how great is the potential negative impact here and accordingly the need for action? Who else could deal with this situation (last resort)? Are we able to deal with it (capability and proximity)? In other words, can we use the Kew Gardens Principles to help others see this decision as their responsibility, rather than passing the buck?

The point is that this argument about locus of responsibility—"This is not my problem, or I'm just following orders"—is often used when folks already know they are uncomfortable with a decision or action but are afraid of the consequences of voicing and acting on that judgment. The argument is not that the act itself is "right" but rather that they are not the appropriate individuals or do not possess the authority to deal with it. Therefore, the individuals using this argument have already acknowledged that they don't like the situation, and this provides an opening for further discussion.

Finally, with regard to the "locus of loyalty" arguments, we noted earlier that the question and definition of loyalty can be framed in multiple ways. For example, are we "loyal" when we protect the current financial bonus of our team by distorting the revenue recognition principle in the quarterly report, or when we protect their long-term reputation and productivity by resisting?

Once we begin to recognize these categories of rationalization or argument, we can also start to recognize patterns in the way we can reframe and reason through the rationalizations, and then craft responses to them. These patterns become a set of tools we can use, again and again, as we confront values conflicts. For example, when we face workplace challenges to our values, our choices are often framed as "false dichotomies," pitting idealism against nihilism. One of the most stubborn underlying assumptions in rationalizations of ethically questionable behavior is that a reasonable (and "pragmatic") aversion to self-destructive behavior is a justification for *any* behavior. To illustrate, some might cite an unforgiving market as the reason for all sorts of financial reporting distortions and operating manipulations. If the market does not tolerate the trade-off of short-term profits for long-term gain in one instance, then this becomes an excuse to abandon the attempt to forge open, honest communications in any instance. This kind of false dichotomy—between unquestioning moral idealism on the one hand and a suspension of all obligations on the other—is often the subtext behind justifications for unethical behavior. However, it usually obscures a more complex reality.

Recognizing and unpacking false dichotomies is just one common lever for responding to frequently heard rationalizations. Other such levers include:

- *Think in the long run as well as the short run.* Notice that the point here is not to abandon the short term for the long term (another sort of false dichotomy), but rather to put them into dialogue with each other, making the true costs and trade-offs of a decision more evident.
- Consider the situation in terms of the group and the firm's *wider purpose,* rather than of the immediate transaction alone. For example, what behavior enables us to serve our customers best; to manage ourselves most efficiently; to manage ourselves in the most honest manner; to align

incentives of the firm, the sales team, and the customers?

- Consider and question our *assumed definition of "competitive advantage."* This definition sometimes seems to reflect the old joke about two lawyers pursued by a bear in the woods. One lawyer says to the other, "We'll never be able to outrun that bear," and the other replies, "I don't have to outrun that bear; I just have to outrun you." Implicit in this view of competitiveness is the assumption that the purpose of business is conquest, narrowly defined as outrunning the competitors (whether this means the firm's external competition or our own competitors for a choice promotion within the firm). This model often results in shortsighted, narrow conceptions of managerial purpose. We might consider an alternative definition for competitiveness, based on overall and long-term excellence, rather than merely outrunning the competition. Such a definition can also allow for consideration of *how* we achieve results, as well as whether we do so.

- Position ourselves as *agents of "continuous improvement" and actionable alternatives,* as opposed to the source of complaints and "thou shalt not's." For example, in

Chapter 4, Frank could ask, "How can we improve this system of incentives and goals to maximize performance while discouraging gaming the system? And in particular, as a member of the audit team, how can I represent your interests there?" rather than simply railing against the distortion of the sales reports.

- Point out *addictive cycles* that can cause greater and greater pressures and risks, leading to larger and larger values conflicts. That is, once we set expectations of a certain type of behavior or certain levels of inauthentic and perhaps unrealistic performance, the pressure to maintain that behavior or even exceed those levels becomes ever greater.

- Point out the *limitations of the game metaphor* in business. A frequently heard rationalization for unethical behavior is to suggest that this is just the way the game is played. And there are ways in which business activities and games are similar, but there are very important ways in which they are different. For example, it can be useful to ask, "What is the time frame for the decision or action under consideration?" An hour's game is very different from an ongoing business activity with impacts that are similarly long lasting. Similarly, asking "What is at stake?" can emphasize the distinctions between a business and a game of entertainment. Additional important questions that can emphasize the limits of the game metaphor include: What are the goals? Do all the participants know the rules? Is participation in the activity freely chosen? Are third parties (people not directly involved in the activity) affected?

- Consider the *costs to each affected party* and look for ways to recognize and mitigate these to make our arguments more appealing. This is what we are after when we ask what is at stake for all concerned. Understanding what is at stake for our target audience can help us to frame the most effective arguments. At a minimum, acknowledging these stakes can sometimes defuse our audience's sense that we are naive or unrealistic.

- Assume our target audience members are *pragmatists* (as opposed to idealists or opportunists) and look for ways to make it feel feasible to them to do the right thing. This does not mean that they will never pay a price for their choices (sometimes such choices do mean sacrifice, at least in the short run), but it means that they will not feel as if they have been exploited for doing so. In Chapter 7, when Susan persuaded her boss to refrain from distorting the performance benchmarks for their client's investment portfolio, she offered him such reasons and arguments that made it easier for him to live with that choice. She had developed some ways to explain the less than stellar results that were likely to be acceptable to the client and that protected her boss from personal blame.

- Assuming our audience members are pragmatists, we will also need to *counter the commonly held assumption of unethical behavior.* That is, pragmatists often expect the lowest common denominator of behavior from those around them. In order to motivate individuals to step beyond this lowest common denominator, it is useful to share examples of effective managers who have made choices based on their sense of responsibility. These are those positive examples we talked about earlier.

As explained above, our purpose in identifying and delineating these different categories of rationalization, the levers for responding to rationalizations, as well as the categories of values dilemmas, is to help us recognize them when we encounter them, to understand the ways of thinking that produce them, and to be practiced in responding to them. So let's look at an example of how this might work. Consider the story of Jonathan.[6]

Jonathan works as an engineering manager in the product group for a leading computer systems company. He recently learned, through informal conversation with some of his colleagues, that the firm's single-wipe hard-drive reconfiguration process is failing five percent of the time. This means that customers can be purchasing reconditioned hard drives that still have the previous owner's data on them. He and his colleagues speculate that it could cost upward of $5 million to address this glitch with the reconfiguration process, so no one really wants to name or "own" the problem. After all, there have been no complaints outside the company and this has probably been going on for at least six months.

Still, Jonathan is uncomfortable. He is worried not only about meeting the expectations of customers who have paid for a clean system, but also about the violation of privacy of the previous owners of these systems. It's just not a product situation he can feel good about.

Ideally, Jonathan would like to get his colleagues to take up the concern in the organization together with him. He thinks it will have more impact that way. On the other hand, no one wants to be the one to break this news. Especially since there have been recent cutbacks, money is tight, and no one wants to have to charge more against their group's expenses. At least for now, it feels to folks in his group that "ignorance is bliss." And no one expects to be thanked for calling attention to the problem. The question is: who will be blamed if it surfaces?

What can Jonathan say, to whom, when, and how?

To help Jonathan with his pre-scripting, we can start by considering what are the main arguments he is trying to counter. What are the reasons and rationalizations he needs to address? These might include:

- This is not really my problem, because I don't work directly on this reconfiguration process, or because I didn't personally see the reconfiguration problem, or because . . .
- And although it's not really my problem, I am likely to have to pay the price if I bring it up by taking charges against my group's expenses, or bearing the brunt of my colleagues' resentment.
- There are enough links in this chain that the problem is not necessarily going to come back to us. Customers may not even realize they have the data on their systems.
- It's not likely that customers will have any way or ability to exploit the previous owner's data, even if they do find it.
- It doesn't compromise the functioning of the product the customer purchased.
- Other arguments, reasons, rationalizations?

Then we will want to consider what is at stake for the key parties, including those with whom Jonathan disagrees. For example:

- For the previous owners, their privacy is at stake.
- For the new owners, their reasonable expectation or right to a "clean" machine without the clutter of previous owners' data is at stake.
- For the company, its reputation with customers for quality, reliability, and respect for customer privacy is at stake.
- For Jonathan and his colleagues, they face a potential increase in their group expenses to fix the problem, as well as a potential lack of receptivity from those higher up in the firm who don't want to hear about such problems.
- Jonathan risks his relationship with colleagues as well as superiors.
- Jonathan and his colleagues risk their sense of integrity and pride in their product.
- Other issues at stake?

Finally we can think about how Jonathan might use the levers described above to develop a script to influence his target audiences in the firm. For example, some arguments might include:

- Think in the long run as well as the short run: in the long run, for example, the firm, the team, and the consumers may bear the burden of increased costs incurred due to compromised systems; privacy violation complaints; liability; reputation costs; loss of future sales; and so on.
- Consider the situation in terms of the group and the firm's wider purpose: what behavior enables them to serve their customers best (by providing the best quality product, for example); to maintain positive long-term relationships with customers; to address limitations in their product reconfiguration processes in a timely manner; to manage their team in the most efficient manner; to manage themselves in the most honest manner; to align incentives of the firm, their own group, and the customers?
- Watch out for false dichotomies. Although the company is experiencing cutbacks and urging cost cutting, that does not mean that executives would consider any expense (in this case, fixing the glitch) to be worth the accompanying risk (customer outrage and loss of reputation).
- Position oneself as an agent of "continuous improvement" as opposed to a source of complaint. Can Jonathan frame this

situation as on "ongoing risk" and use it as an opportunity to recommend a systematic improvement, thereby reframing the present cost against both present and future return?

- Point out addictive cycles that can cause greater and greater pressures and risks. As above, Jonathan can point out that this is not an isolated problem but arguably something that can present ongoing challenges.

- Consider who is needed as an ally, as opposed to an adversary: for example, rather than painting colleagues into a corner by going over their heads, Jonathan can try to enlist them in his efforts. Similarly, he can try to find ways to work with the group's manager, helping to develop arguments to use when reporting the higher costs incurred in fixing the problem.

- Assume the target audience is composed of pragmatists (as opposed to idealists or opportunists) and look for ways to make it feasible for them to do the right thing. If Jonathan assumes his colleagues are pragmatists, he will need to counter the commonly held assumption of unethical behavior: that is, pragmatists often will expect the lowest common denominator of behavior in those around them. In order to motivate his colleagues to step beyond this limitation, Jonathan could point to examples of effective managers who have made choices based on their values. Can Jonathan point to such examples in the firm?

These are just a few ways that Jonathan might use our list of levers to help him craft his script for voicing values in the workplace. Now let's look at another source of tools and arguments for building scripts: research on decision-making biases and heuristics. A useful place to start is a relatively brief and readable essay by Robert Prentice that summarizes a great deal of psychological research on common decision rules and biases that can sometimes result in less than optimal or even unethical choices. Prentice's stated objective is to help educators place future business practitioners "on guard" against these tendencies. He acknowledges at the end of his essay, as we have noted earlier, that some research has indicated that mere awareness of decision biases does not protect us against them, although it may make us more aware of the tendencies in others. Nevertheless, he notes that others have had some success in a sort of inoculation against such errors in decision making.[7]

We, however, have a very different use in mind for Prentice's compilation of research findings. That is, by understanding these decision-making tendencies, we can be better able to unpack and respond to the reasons and rationalizations proffered by *others* for taking an action that violates our own values. We may be better able to see through those arguments and create persuasive scripts for responding to them, because we can frame our counterarguments in ways that name and thereby reduce the power of these decision-making biases. And we can even use an awareness of these biases to frame our own positions in ways that make them more appealing or persuasive. And even if we are unable to change the minds of those who presented the rationalizations, by offering convincing arguments we may be able to strengthen the resolve of others who feel as we do and wish to counter the questionable behavior, too.

One of the assumptions here is that we are more likely to find the courage and commitment to act on our own values if we can find the words to express them persuasively, to ourselves as well as to others. This assumption is based on the observation that often the first step toward acting on our values is the willingness to "go public" with their expression. And alternatively, if we do not express our values, it unfortunately becomes easier to act as if they were never ours to begin with.

In the service of enhancing our scripts then, let's look at the list of thirteen decision tendencies and biases identified by Prentice that may affect ethical choices. The summary below defines them very briefly, but adds suggestions for using them proactively as tools for voicing our values, rather than simply reactively as effects to guard against. These suggestions are intended to transform Prentice's list of risks into a list of potential tools as well.

## Obedience to Authority

Citing the famous Milgram experiments, Prentice describes the proven tendency to obey those in authority, suggesting that we should be on guard against this predilection. However, it might also be useful to consider, when trying to develop effective strategies for voicing our values, whether there are alternate authorities that we might reference in our scripts (our boss's boss, for example, or the industry codes of conduct rather than our firm's common practice, or the applicable government regulations).

We might also attempt to defuse the power of this tendency by naming it. That is, we might acknowledge that we are mindful and respectful of the fact that our boss is more experienced and has more authority within the organization, but that the issue is so important, or we have collected so much contrary information, that we nevertheless feel the need to raise it. In this way we acknowledge deference to authority even as we gently push against it. This is a strategy that Lisa Baxter used very well, as we saw in Chapter 7.

## Social Proof

Here Prentice cites research demonstrating that our very
thinking is sometimes influenced and altered by the context in which we operate. Irving Janis called this phenomenon "groupthink."[8] Again we might try to defuse
this pressure somewhat by naming it and thereby calling
it into question (for example, "I wonder why we all have
coalesced around this decision so quickly. Are there no
counterarguments we should consider?"). Or we might
try to build a coalition of like-minded individuals (either
inside or outside the organization), to thereby alter the
social context from which we derive our sense of "proof."
That is, construct an alternative group to help us see
more positions and from which to draw reinforcement.
This is, of course, one of the arguments for engaging
multiple stakeholders when confronting complex and
high-impact decisions.

One senior managing director in a major financial
services firm reported that early in his career he and his
wife had discussed the high-risk nature of his business,
and he told her he would rather be fired than violate his
own values. Sharing this position early on may help to
head off the bind that many have described experiencing
later in their careers, when they feel alone with their ethical choices and fear that their family will be negatively
affected by their decisions. Instead this executive made
his family another important social context that could
help him derive confidence and support rather than

pressure, as well as affirmation or "social proof" of his perspective on the ethical infractions he might encounter. This is a similar approach to Denise Foley's decision to challenge her CEO, when her conversations with her husband and other colleagues helped her to develop an alternative social context for assessing the situation.

## False Consensus Effect

Research suggests that we tend to believe others will think as we do: if we think something is unethical, we are likely to believe others will as well. On the other hand, if we tend toward cynicism, we may expect the worst in all situations, whether it is warranted or not.

In general, this finding suggests that it is useful to assume nothing and always test our conclusions with others, both as a check on our own possible blind spots and as a way to accurately assess our support or lack thereof in the organization. That is, just as our superiors or peers may not always be as honest as we expect them to be, they may not always be as cynical either. If we assume that everyone is ethical, we may become vulnerable to manipulation, but if we assume that everyone is unethical, we may feel unnecessarily discouraged in our efforts to voice our values.[9] And if we assume that our initial conclusion about what is right or wrong is generally shared, we may be surprised by the resistance we encounter. Finally, as with most of the biases discussed in Prentice's paper, naming this tendency toward "false consensus" can be a useful way to open a conversation, helping our target audience understand that their assumptions about what may or may not be possible are not necessarily shared by all.

It bears mentioning that the false-consensus effect may at first glance appear to contradict our susceptibility to social proof. The first effect suggests we tend to believe that others think as we do, whereas the second suggests that our own conclusions are often influenced by the perspectives of others, sometimes unduly. Aside from simply acknowledging that people are complex and not always consistent, it is helpful to recognize that false consensus is often a going-in assumption—the starting point for our thinking—whereas social proof is based on experience and context.

## Overoptimism

As Prentice reminds us, and as we saw with Denise Foley, research suggests that our optimism can lead to irrational choices: for example, "we will make these sales numbers even though they may appear aggressive," or "we will not get caught." When crafting responses to rationalizations for unethical behavior that are based on overoptimism, we may be inclined to interrogate the factual basis for the arguments, marshaling counterarguments when possible. Given this human tendency, however, it may also be helpful to appeal to the optimism of our listeners by positing scenarios of how ethical decision making can help the firm succeed. That is, it is useful not only to question irrational optimism but also to proffer something positive in its place.

## Self-Serving Bias

Research supports the idea that people tend to look for information that will confirm preexisting views, to interpret information in ways that support their own view, and to selectively remember the information that supports their view. As with all the biases described here, we do well to consider the ramifications of this tendency for our own judgments as well as those of others, but again research suggests that awareness of this tendency alone does not necessarily make us proof against it.

Accordingly, one strategy that group leaders or individuals among peers might undertake is to construct a kind of thought experiment, wherein the team is invited to generate and support alternate interpretations of the same data. This process may generate some persuasive arguments and serve to soften the ground for our efforts to persuade listeners to consider a different, perhaps less self-serving interpretation. As with all of the tools described here, this approach may be used for good or ill: that is, to support ethical as well as unethical positions. The point here is that we want to tap into the full range of argumentation and persuasive strategies at our dis-

posal when voicing our values, rather than relying exclusively on seeming self-righteous assertions.


## Framing

Research has shown that responses to the same choice
may be quite different depending on how the question is
framed. For example, Prentice reminds us, "People's risk
preferences change dramatically depending on whether
an option is framed in terms of potential loss or potential gain," with potential gain being favored.[10]

Once again, this observation can be useful because
it helps us to deconstruct and see through the framing that may be applied to make an unethical choice appear necessary or even ethical, and also because it suggests a powerful tool that we may utilize as we frame our
proposed alternative action choices. We can frame our
choices not only in terms of potential negative consequences avoided (possible legal or regulatory problems,
for example) in an effort to adhere to our values, but also
in terms of positive benefits achieved (greater team cohe-
sion, increased motivation, improved brand value).

It is important to remember that framing (like all the
tools and biases described here) can be an extremely powerful tool, and as noted previously, it can be used for a variety of purposes, for better or worse ends. A useful perspective to maintain when consciously considering ways
to reframe an argument is that our intent is to enable lis-

teners to see a position clearly, and that means we want to help them see our own position just as clearly and persuasively as they may already see the position we find unethical. However, in the end, we understand that individuals will make their own decisions, guided by their own values and priorities. We are not attempting to "manipulate" or trick them into accepting a particular point of view. Instead we invite listeners to see that they have more choices than they may have thought, and that they do, in fact, have the option to act on their values if they so choose. If we attempt to use reframing as a means to manipulate others into accepting our position, we invite a kind of escalating "war of frames" and an accompanying cynicism.

To the contrary, the encouragement of voice in the workplace suggests that we would welcome the opportunity to test our values-based positions in an open dialogue. After all, we are just as prone to decision-making biases as our audiences. This stance is not the same as relativism; we are not arguing that every choice is as good as every other one. Rather we are saying that when we voice our values, the goal is to present our position in a way that reveals it to be as feasible and as persuasive as possible and that clearly demonstrates our conviction.

## Process

Prentice refers to research about the often described "slippery slope"—that is, the tendency for people to willingly take certain actions that they would have found objectionable had they not been eased into them through a series of smaller, less extreme choices. These small choices make the bigger choice appear less objectionable in context. Prentice, of course, suggests that this insight is useful for placing us on guard against corporate cultures that can make unethical choices appear normal and even expected.

But this tendency is also useful in thinking about ways to make *positive* impacts in an organization. In a powerful article, "Small Wins: Redefining the Scale of Social Problems," Karl Weick argues: "People often define social problems in ways that overwhelm their ability to do anything about them. . . . When the magnitude of problems is scaled upward in the interest of mobilizing action, the quality of thought and action declines, because processes such as frustration, arousal, and helplessness are activated." Weick suggests a more positive vision of the slippery slope: "A series of wins at small but significant tasks . . . reveals a pattern that may attract allies, deter opponents, and lower resistance to subsequent proposals."[11] It can be helpful to find ways of breaking down challenges to our values into smaller, more immediately actionable steps, rather than asking our colleagues to "change the system" all at once.

## Cognitive Dissonance

Similar to the self-serving bias, the urge to avoid cognitive dissonance gives us a tendency to rule out information or conclusions that make us uncomfortable because they conflict with already accepted positions. Colleagues and bosses are just as susceptible to this bias as we are. Building an appreciation for contradiction and constructive challenges into the corporate culture may be a useful organizational response to this tendency, and on an individual level, we can practice explicitly inviting alternative viewpoints. It may be useful to assemble a network of trusted advisers that includes folks with whom we often disagree but whose intelligence and integrity we respect.

But we can also use this insight to help us more effectively voice our values. When we try to change the minds of individuals who may be protecting their own prior decisions, we can trigger this kind of cognitive dissonance in them. They may be tempted to rule out any input because it makes them uncomfortable with their previous choices. In such a case, it may be useful to find ways to affirm and support other positions they have taken, giving them a sense of continuity with one aspect of themselves even as we are threatening another.

This is what Lisa Baxter did when the chairman of her company's board objected to her decision to fire an executive to whom he was committed. She was successful in defending her differences with the chairman's assessment of the executive by appealing to another decision the chairman had already taken, to approve a new strategic agenda for the firm. His initial reluctance to accept a negative view of an executive whom he had supported was resolved into his commitment to another, more powerful position he had also "owned."

## Sunk Costs and Loss Aversion

Prentice reports research on our tendency to continue with a less than optimal course of action simply because we are reluctant to accept that our previous choices or investments were wrong or wasted, or because "people detest losses more than they enjoy gains, about twice as much."[12]

When trying to persuade individuals to change their minds about a decision that conflicts with our values, we may encounter their reluctance to change course because they have already invested time or resources into their prior positions. It may be useful to talk about what we have already gained from the prior decision or investment, even if it's not the gain they anticipated. We may have other "returns" we can point out, whether they are knowledge, relationships, or something else. We may also use stories of how other firms have benefited from similar mistakes, providing an alternative way to view the previous decision, such as, it was a valuable lesson, a growth experience. In other words, we can try to provide a way of viewing the previous decision as already having paid off, so we are freer to move on, at a point when it is no longer viable or, in the context of this discussion, ethical.

In a related observation, organizational scholar Chris Argyris describes managers' tendency toward "defensive reasoning" in a classic article from the *Harvard Business Review,* explaining: "Defensive reasoning encourages individuals to keep private the premises, inferences, and conclusions that shape their behavior and to avoid testing them in a truly independent, objective fashion."[13] Argyris observes that this behavior is born out of a view that we are either winners or losers, in control or controlled, and that there-fore, in an effort to protect ourselves from perspectives that may threaten our perceived status, we become closed off from new information or points of view. His intent is to illustrate how this approach leads to poor decisions because it precludes learning (which by definition is about engag-ing with new ideas, different from the ones we came in with). For our purposes, these observations illustrate why some people might be closed toward our efforts to voice our values, and they suggest that it can be effective to frame these efforts as about "learning" and new information that can enhance all of our decision making.

## The Tangible, the Abstract, and the Time-Delay Traps

Research argues that "vivid, tangible, contemporaneous factors" affect our choices more powerfully than those that are "removed in time and space."[14] Research also supports our usual preference for immediate rather than delayed gratification. As Prentice illustrates, it can be "difficult to decide to pull the plug on a product (even a Ford Pinto or a Dalkon Shield), lay off employees work-ing on the product, and damage the company's profits in the short term when the potential injuries are hypothetical at this point, temporally-distant, and again, will be visited upon merely statistical victims."[15]

When voicing our values involves confronting these tendencies, the challenge becomes to somehow make the distant seem near, the statistics feel like real individuals, and the hypothetical appear as concrete as strong odds can make it. The use of analogies or actual stories from our own firm's or other firms' experience may be helpful, and the more similar the situation the better, of course. In interviews with managers who had effectively voiced their values in the workplace, they often said that they had used compelling stories, visual aids like decision trees, or quantitative analyses to make their arguments feel more tangible and impactful. Of course, not every approach works with every audience. In his book on how we can "change minds," for example, Howard Gardner notes that stories are particularly useful in attempting to influence large, diverse groups, while theories can be used in communicating with smaller, more homogeneous groups, and that interpersonal insights and skills are critical when addressing individuals personally.[16]

So let's look at how we might actually use some of the tools we have derived from these insights about decision-making biases in an attempt to voice our values. If we re-visit the story of Denise Foley and her decision to challenge the CEO's plan to sell their nonprofit hospital to a for-profit institution—a plan whose implications, in Foley's view, went well beyond the financial and threatened the well-being of the community the hospital served—

we can consider how her reasoning and her arguments might be informed by an understanding of the kinds of decision biases to which she and her CEO are most vulnerable.

To begin with, Foley certainly feels the pressure, internal and external, to offer her obedience to authority, in this case the CEO. An internal strategy for checking this tendency within herself is to note that there are multiple and different relevant authorities in this situation and to thereby place them all in play. In this way, Foley determines which is most salient and appropriate: the authority of her boss, the authority of the institution's mission, the authority of her own conscience, and so on. And she can craft her arguments so that they reflect that determination.

An external strategy for responding to this bias toward obedience to authority is to name it: when speaking to the CEO or others in the hospital, to acknowledge that she is aware and respectful of the boss, his experience and authority, but that this issue is so important that it must still be raised. In this way, she anticipates the charge of insubordination and places her discussion on a different level.

Foley is also subject to the pressure of social proof, wherein the certainty and united front of the CEO and the consultant might influence her to second-guess her own opinion. One strategy Foley uses is to check her viewpoint with some respected and trusted peers inside and outside the organization. The trick is to find individuals she can speak candidly with and who will be honest with her as well as respect the confidentiality of the query. They must be folks who are not easily influenced and who keep their own counsel. In this way, Foley is creating her own social context, whether it is her family or close friends outside the hospital or respected peers within.

The CEO himself may be vulnerable to the false consensus effect, believing that others would agree with him, largely because his only real source of input is the consultant he has hired himself. He has isolated himself from the CFO and he is still relatively new to the organization, which has had an embattled recent past. A useful strategy for Foley can be to name the CEO's relative isolation and share some carefully selected and credible alternative viewpoints, her own among them.

Foley can also counter the overoptimism to which the CEO may be vulnerable regarding the likely ultimate outcome of selling the hospital. She could bring in stories as well as data on the outcomes of similar transactions, borrowing a lesson from Gardner, who argues that communicating your point in multiple formats (such as data in addition to stories) can make it more likely to influence your listener.

The consultant may be vulnerable to a self-serving bias, rather than consciously intending to mislead the CEO. It can be useful for Foley to proceed from this assumption, rather than accusing the consultant of duplicity. Whether or not the consultant is conscious of his errors, presenting her arguments in this way may make it easier for the CEO to hear them. Instead of accusing the very adviser the CEO has handpicked, thereby possibly embarrassing the CEO or engaging his tendency to defend a past choice (sunk costs), Foley can proceed as if she assumes both are operating in good faith, and that they simply are lacking some information that she can provide.

The framing that Foley uses to communicate with the CEO is critical. Instead of positioning herself as right and the CEO as wrong, for example, she can frame the choice as a data-driven decision over which two talented individuals who respect each other may disagree, particularly if one of them has incomplete or inaccurate data. Then her task becomes one of bringing more accurate and complete data to bear, rather than proving her boss wrong.

The framing of her argument is also important when she tells the CEO that she cannot support the decision to sell the hospital. When she frames her own position as based in her conviction that other employees will be able to read her discomfort, thereby undermining her effectiveness as a manager and leader, as opposed to framing her position as a rejection of the CEO, she is better able to deal with her own reluctance to seem disloyal and to prevent the CEO from seeing her that way. Given her respect for and positive relationship with the CEO, framing her argument as an appeal to their shared goal of saving the hospital and serving the health-care needs of the community is a useful way of placing them on the same side when she approaches him.

The point is that all of these biases, which we and our target audiences are mutually vulnerable to, can also be viewed as ways to anticipate and understand the resistance we are likely to face and to craft the most effective arguments and responses to them. Rather than view these decision-making biases as dangers only, we can consciously choose to name and own them and use them to deconstruct our own and our audience's first tendencies if and when they are less than rational or less than ethical.

As with all of the discussions in this book—defining purpose, normalizing values conflicts, identifying preferred communications styles and strengths, and so on—the pattern is to recognize and name the reality not because we can necessarily change it but so that we can use it to our advantage when we try to voice our values. The point is to see things as they are but also to realize that we do have some choices about how we respond to them. So in this chapter we have examined a whole series of decision-making biases and frequently used rationalizations for less than ethical choices, so that we might take control of them, use them to our advantage by mining them for our persuasive ores to reinforce our values scripts.

## CHAPTER NINE

# Putting It to Work

In his classic book of the same title, Albert O. Hirschman posits three potential responses to decline in nations or organizations: exit, voice, and loyalty.[1] If we think back to the categories of responses to values conflicts identified by those MBA students we talked about, they also fall into these categories. Some students just did what they were told (a form of loyalty, although its focus is questionable); some removed themselves from the situation; and some found a way to express their values, sometimes successfully, in an effort to change the situation for the better. The Giving Voice to Values approach to thinking about and enacting our values is informed by Hirschman's observation, and focuses on making the exercise of voice more likely, more comfortable, and more apt to be effective. We do this by naming and sharing examples of our own and others' successful exercise of voice, by analyzing those examples as well as relevant research for models and approaches to build our tool kit, by understanding our own strengths and predilections so we can play to them, and finally by providing the impetus and the opportunity to practice our voice and our scripts.

In the previous chapters we looked deeply at a set of concepts and tactics with the goals of expanding the "enablers" for voicing our values and counteracting or transforming the "disablers." We identified seven pillars or foundational concepts and explored one in each chapter: Values; Choice; Normality; Purpose; Self-Knowledge, Self-Image, and Alignment; Voice; and Reasons and Rationalizations. Taken together, these pillars are a kind of action framework or "to-do list" for voicing our values. But there are some broader insights and observations that have become clear over the years from research and interviews with individuals about times they have acted on their values, as well as times they have failed to do so. It seems appropriate to mention these observations here, as we conclude this book.

First, counterintuitive as it may seem, *the arguments we use to voice our values need not be entirely unassailable and perfect.* As discussed earlier, we sometimes hesitate or even stop ourselves from voicing our values because the arguments for *not* doing so seem so sharp and clear. But taking the time to analyze those arguments and craft credible responses to them has been a major focus of the preceding pages, and we have seen that those seemingly flawless arguments for why we cannot voice our values are also imperfect. In other words, although an understanding of the uses of language and framing and decision-making biases can certainly help us to unpack and see through the arguments we want to counter, as well as construct arguments that will be persuasive in response, the bottom line is that these are all just tools. As we have seen, they can be used more or less skillfully and for good or ill.

The importance of this insight cannot be overestimated, but it can easily be misunderstood. It is not to say that any perspective is just as good as any other, but rather that the arguments we use to support those perspectives can be strengthened or weakened by our ability to use the tools of analysis and persuasion, just as statistics can be interpreted and presented in many different ways. Sometimes these different uses are intentional distortions, but sometimes they are simply choices to place value on one set of criteria over another. Our intention in this book is the latter: to help our listeners entertain a version of their reality that prioritizes a different set of criteria than the ones with which they may have come into the conversation.

Therefore, recognizing that someone else may create another set of arguments that support a different viewpoint is no longer a reason to bite our tongues. Our arguments may be imperfect, but so are theirs. Their arguments are based on a set of assumptions about the purpose of business, or of their own work, that are not necessarily universal. The point is to offer a story line, a narrative that enables those of us who want to voice and enact a set of shared values in the workplace that prioritizes integrity and compassion and a commitment to organizational practices that support those values. Too often, individuals who want to voice and act on their values don't feel they have a credible story to tell, and we need that story from which to draw confidence, so we will be able to articulate those priorities to others as well as to ourselves.

The scripts and arguments that are used by individuals who voice their values are not magic bullets. They are often surprisingly familiar. But in the stories we have considered, the point is that they were in fact *spoken*. The Giving Voice to Values approach is designed to make it more likely that we can all actually speak these scripts because we have crafted them in advance and, importantly, because we have practiced voicing them.

The second general observation is that *when we confront values conflicts at work, we typically reflect on the risks associated with voicing our values, but individuals who did voice their values tended to reflect on the risks associated with not doing so.* They were concerned about whether they could live with themselves, or what kinds of escalating pressures they would face further down the line if they succumbed now, or whether they could convincingly lead their subordinates in a direction they did not agree with, or what the negative implications for their customers or their investors would be. If we entertain only the downside of one course of action (voicing our values) and only the upside of another (not voicing our values), no wonder it may be difficult to find the confidence to speak up.

Third, it is useful to be open to the power of surprise. *Sometimes the most effective arguments we can craft*

*in the service of our values are the ones we least expect.*
When the issue at stake is linked to our deepest values,
we sometimes feel as if we need to go immediately to that
place of righteous and passionate appeal to morality and
ethics. However, sometimes the most persuasive and constructive appeals are much simpler and less emotional.

For example, a government administrator in India
who was responsible for land usage and construction issues in his district was faced with a local conflict when
the majority Hindu community started to construct an
expansion of its temple onto land that was owned by a
businessman who happened to be Muslim.[2] It was a clear
violation of his legal ownership, but it was also an election
year and local politicians were interested in the support of
the voting majority. The civil servant himself was committed to upholding the law but was also concerned about
potential unrest that could be triggered if either party
wanted to politicize the issue by appealing to its own religious community. What's more, the temple was an ancient
and important spiritual site and the administrator's own
family was very concerned about protecting it from possible damage that might result from heightened conflict.

Despite all the conflicting priorities and motivations, the administrator, although personally committed
to the rule of law that he believed was only fair and essential for his region to prosper, framed his negotiations
in a very pragmatic fashion. He was therefore able to
recognize the businessman's motivations: that is, that he
had no desire for escalated conflict and no need to pun-

ish the temple committee even though it was clearly in violation of the law. The landowner wanted to maintain reasonable relations with the community where he did business. Therefore, the civil servant managed to negotiate a peaceful agreement, protecting the owner's legal rights but also persuading him to help the temple committee to cover its costs for new construction on their own land. The administrator's openness to seeing the issue through different lenses—political, religious, economic, legal—and his willingness to question his and others' assumptions about everyone's motivations allowed him to recognize unexpected but effective approaches to the affected parties.

Underscoring the importance of this observation, research tells us that we are often incorrect when we assign motivations to others. "People have a pervasive tendency to attribute another individual's behavior to that individual's disposition, rather than to situational factors," according to Andrew Molinsky and Joshua Margolis; on the other hand, they also are likely "to attribute negative outcomes of their own behavior to situational factors."[3] That is, although we tend to assume that other people are just wrong or even bad when they act unethically, we assume that when we ourselves do so, we are trapped or forced into taking such actions. As we saw with the Indian administrator above, it is useful to ask:

- What assumptions are we making about the values and the motivations of our-

selves and others, as well as about the situational limits we each face, when we encounter values conflicts?

- How would our view of the situation change
  if we questioned those assumptions?
- Even if we are convinced that we are correct about our assumptions, how would
  we act differently if we held different
  assumptions?

This last question is an example of the Giving Voice
to Values approach to such conflicts, because it invites us
to think about what might enable us to feel *as if* we had
more choices. That is, what changes in not only the external conditions, but also in our sense of our priorities
and of our abilities and tendencies might help us to act?
And in turn, would we see things that we could change
that might enable the other person to feel and act as if
they also had more choices, just as the administrator created more choices for the temple committee by getting
the builder to agree to help them with their costs?

Fourth, although values conflicts often come with
time pressure attached, and often individuals feel they
have only one shot to respond to them—that is, it's now
or never—*we have nevertheless learned of some clever
ways to buy time for our response.* Time pressures, real or
imagined, often play into our belief that we have a choice
(or not) to voice and enact our values. Responding to
values conflicts often requires creativity, and in her re-

search on creativity, Teresa Amabile tells us that extreme time pressure can often create challenges for creative thinking. She has found notable exceptions, however, such as when we can engender a feeling of being on a vital mission, and when we can find and protect spans of time for uninterrupted work or thinking.[4]

We saw how Jeff Salett found a way to resist the immediate pressure to distort his firm's financial reporting by developing a program to promote integrity across the firm and imbuing it with a sense of criticality and significance, enlisting the support of the CEO and using his new position as a moment for making change. He engaged his organization in a "vital mission," and thereby bought time to address the problems that had created the pressures to distort the firm's financial restructuring charges.

Our interviews with individuals who have voiced their values included folks who, while unable to figure out a way to speak in the moment, did find a way to bring the issue up again later. One manager was taken off guard when an issue came up in a meeting with all the senior executives and a decision was taken immediately that conflicted with her values. Although she had not been able to muster the words or the confidence to speak in the moment, she left a message with her boss shortly after the meeting, saying that she had some follow-up thoughts that she believed were significant and asking for a moment of his time to discuss them. She then used this "found time" to muster her creative thinking and prepare both a written and a verbal script, drawing on her own best communication traits as well as her familiarity with what her boss tended to find persuasive, and she was able to make an effective case. Of course, although she did not speak in the moment, it was important that she did not wait too long before creating another opportunity to make her arguments.[5]

The fifth observation here has to do with courage. We have already seen how some people believe the driving force behind a decision to voice their values is their identity as a cautious or even fearful person, while others think it is their identity as a risk taker or bold leader. Nevertheless, many of us—perhaps most—think that courage or at least confidence is a useful if not necessary trait for voicing our values, even if it is not the driving force. However, we have also learned that *courage is defined and triggered by different things for different people: that is, each of us can choose to define courage in a way that allows us to access it more easily, given our own strengths and preferences.*

Consider the following two examples. In an account of a daring escape from the concentration camps in Nazi Germany, the survivors explained that they found the courage to act in such desperate conditions and against such overwhelming odds, not because they were optimistic, but because they absolutely believed that the alternative was unbearable. In a sense, they acted because they had lost all hope for surviving their current situation.[6]

On the other hand, a successful author and speaker who teaches and gives presentations for hundreds of people says that she overcomes her anxiety and fear of standing in front of these crowds precisely because she *has* hope. That is, each time she goes to speak, she has hope that she will be able to make a positive difference in the lives of her audience.

For many, the most powerful "courage enabler" is the recognition of what truly is at stake. We can do almost anything in the service of a purpose that is important enough because it is in those instances that we can recognize the true power and influence of our choices.[7] Consider the civil rights activists, or the passive resisters and followers of Gandhi in India, or the courage of an Iraqi lawyer who told U.S. troops how to find the prisoner of war Jessica Lynch at the risk of his own life.

Thus, it seems that one way to enable courage is to know that *not* acting is untenable. The other is to believe that by acting, you can have a positive impact. The former driver comes from pushing away from something— a rejection of the unacceptable status quo; the latter comes from moving toward something with a belief, a confidence in one's own potential power. The point here is that courage is available to all of us. It is only necessary that we consider what works for each of us because courage is triggered by different things for different people.

This book has been all about taking control of our own lives and careers. At heart, it is based on the observation and the conviction that choice exists: that we can choose not only when and how to voice and enact our values but, importantly, how to frame the choices so that we experience more degrees of freedom for doing so.

The preceding chapters offer many perspectives on how to think about and approach values-based conflicts in the workplace, as well as a set of lenses or frameworks by which to view our own encounters with such conflicts in order to expand the competence we feel. However, none of these observations or lenses will be useful unless we actively practice them. They do not make voicing and acting on our values easy in the face of countervailing pressures. They simply expand the sense of possibility.

So here this book concludes with an invitation to be part of a growing cohort of peer coaches in business schools and business organizations around the world who are practicing, mastering, and sharing this powerful Giving Voice to Values thought experiment in ways that empower all of us to more fully, more often, and more effectively voice and act on our values. By asking the questions—"What if we wanted to voice and act on our values? What would we say and do?"—out loud with colleagues and friends, we not only generate scripts and skills for ourselves, but we invite others to be part of our process, building a set of allies who are engaged first simply by helping us to solve *our* problem, with no strings or commitments attached. But once we all begin to work together to craft a response, the barriers begin to feel assailable and our confidence builds. The process of problem solving and peer coaching in itself can create the team.

Most important, dedicating time to focusing on what we would say and do in such situations, and examining the experiences of others who *have* voiced their values, can build the muscle and the instincts to do so as well. Sometimes this determination to speak comes quickly; sometimes it follows much deliberation. But the more we do so (and see others do so), the more we believe we can do so, and the more it becomes a habit, a default position.

In this way we equip ourselves to know not only what is right, but also how to make it happen.

# Appendix

## A. Starting Assumptions for Giving Voice to Values

*Before we begin to practice possible approaches and scripts for voicing our values in the workplace, it is useful to be explicit about our starting assumptions. You may or may not be certain that you share all these assumptions, but in order to gain the most from this approach, it is useful to approach it as if you do. This is the "story line," if you will, behind this work.*

1. **I want to voice and act on my values.**
   Most of us want to find ways to voice and act on our values in the workplace, and to do so effectively.

2. **I have voiced my values at some point in the past.**
   Even though research and our own experiences reveal many individual and organizational inhibitors, most of us have, in fact, chosen to voice and act on our values on some occasions.

3. **I can voice my values more often and more effectively.**
   We have the potential to expand our capacity, effectiveness, and likelihood to voice and act on our values by acknowledging that we have such a choice, and by practicing what we would say and do if we made that choice.

4. **It is easier for me to voice my values in some contexts than others.**
   Developing the "muscle" for voicing our values does not diminish the importance of selecting and developing organizational cultures and policies and incentives that *encourage* such choices. In fact, the effort to promote the development of such cultures, policies, and incentives is, in itself, an instance of voicing values. And the more such organizational enablers are in place, the more likely it is that individuals will choose to voice their values. It is a virtuous circle.

5. **I am more likely to do this if I have practiced how to respond to frequently encountered conflicts.**

   There are certain frequently heard "reasons and rationalizations" for not voicing and acting on our values. But there are also possible responses or reframings that we can use to counter these reasons and rationalizations. If we familiarize ourselves with these responses in advance, we are more likely to be able to access them when needed, potentially shifting a conversation or changing a mind. Prior reflection on responses to value conflicts can expand our confidence in the degrees of freedom we have in any given decision situation.

6. **My example is powerful.**

   Just as we want to voice and act on our values, we can assume that many of our colleagues do as well. If we can access credible counterarguments to frequently heard reasons for not voicing and acting on our values, we may encourage and empower others to join us.

7. **Although mastering and delivering responses to frequently heard rationalizations can empower others who share my views to act, I cannot assume I know who those folks will be.**

   The responses we develop and practice to frequently heard reasons and rationalizations are intended to strengthen our own confidence in voicing and acting on our values, as well as that of others who share our value conflict but are unable to find a way to explain their reluctance. However, we cannot assume we know who feels the conflict and who does not simply by observing their behavior because, as we have already acknowledged, we all have chosen to suppress these "felt" conflicts at some points in our past.

8. **The better I know myself, the more I can prepare to play to my strengths, and, when necessary, protect myself from my weaknesses.**

   The greater our self-knowledge, the more likely we are to be able to anticipate and manage our responses to values conflicts. Prior reflection on our own personalities and behavioral tendencies under pressure enables us to play to our strengths and to put mechanisms in place to protect us from our weaknesses. Research tells us that often these "mechanisms" need to be external (incentives, deterrents, automatic review processes, transparency, a preestablished network of sounding boards). Internal awareness of self-bias is important but not enough to prevent us from falling prey to it: we need to go beyond awareness to action or external mechanisms.

9. **I am not alone.**

   We can utilize our personal support networks as sounding boards; reach out to our colleagues to build a network of allies or gather supporting information; and engage in strategic use of the managerial hierarchy. However, we must consider carefully which approach is most appropriate in a particular situation.

10. **Although I may not always succeed, voicing and acting on my values is worth doing.**

    As with any other managerial action, we do not always succeed at what we set out to achieve. We are more likely to voice our values if we have decided that the cost of not doing so, or the benefit of doing so, is important enough that we would do it whether or not we were successful. In order to get to this place of clarity, we need to spend some serious time thinking about our own identity, personal purpose, and definition of success and failure. It is also important to reflect on the risks associated with voicing our values, so that we make this decision with our eyes open and prepared to handle the risks.

11. **Voicing my values leads to better decisions.**
It is often difficult to be certain that a course of action is "right," but we are more likely to come to the best decision if we feel empowered to voice our concerns about values conflicts and discuss them with others.

12. **The more I believe it's possible to voice and act on my values, the more likely I will be to do so.**
We are more likely to voice and act on our values when we believe it is possible to do so effectively. If we pay attention to positive examples of such voice and action and spend time developing support mechanisms and practicing the development and delivery of responses to frequently heard reasons and rationalizations for unethical actions, we can expand our sense of what's possible—another virtuous circle.

## B. A Tale of Two Stories: An Exercise

*In your career thus far, you have likely encountered workplace situations when your values conflicted with what you were asked to do. Often it is not easy to align your own personal values and purpose with those of your boss, your co-workers, your direct reports, or your firm. This exercise is designed to help you identify and develop the competencies necessary to achieve that alignment.*

### Objectives

1. To reflect on your previous experiences, successful and less so, at effectively voicing and acting on your values in the workplace.
2. To discover which conditions and problem definitions empower you to effectively voice your values, and which tend to inhibit that action.

### *Part I*

Recall a time in your work experience when your values conflicted with what you were expected to do in a particular, nontrivial management decision, and you spoke up and acted to resolve the conflict. Consider the following questions and write down your thoughts and brief responses.

- What did you do, and what was the impact?
- What motivated you to speak up and act?
- How satisfied are you? How would you like to have responded? (This question is not about rejecting or defending past actions but rather about imagining your ideal scenario.)
- What would have made it easier for you to speak or act? Things within your own control? Things within the control of others?

*Part II*

Recall a time in your work experience when your values conflicted with what you were expected to do in a particular,
nontrivial management decision, and you did *not* speak up or
act to resolve the conflict. Consider the following questions and
write down your thoughts and brief responses.

- What happened?
- Why didn't you speak up or act? What would have motivated
  you to do so?
- How satisfied are you? How would you like to have responded?
  (This question is not about rejecting or defending past actions
  but rather about imagining your ideal scenario.)
- What would have made it easier for you to speak/act? Things
  within your own control? Things within the control of others?

*Note:* In this exercise, a "values conflict" refers to a disagreement
that has an ethical dimension to it. That is, I might disagree with
your idea about the most efficient process flow design for an assembly line, but there is usually not an ethical component to
that decision. However, if one design reflected a commitment to
worker safety or environmental concerns and the other didn't, for
example, even this disagreement might be appropriate here.

## C. Enablers for Voicing Values: Some Examples

**What makes it easier to speak and act on our values?**

*Things within our own control*

- Enlisting allies
- Selecting and sequencing of audiences
- Gaining greater confidence in our viewpoint as a result of securing more information
- Starting with questions rather than assertions
- Greater understanding of others' motivations, needs, fears
- Lowering the stress by taking the conversation with dissenters or key supporters off-line, one-on-one, at a mutually convenient time and place
- Working through incremental steps
- Changing the frame of the problem: positioning it as opportunity seeking rather than risk management, for example, or as a "learning dialogue" rather than a reproach
- Finding win-win solutions
- Questioning assumptions, professional rationalizations, and seeming truisms ("The market made me do it"; "I'll behave differently when I'm in charge"; "The invisible hand takes all costs into account so I don't have to"; "Business is a meritocracy so therefore its painful impacts are justified")
- Appealing to shared purpose, values (appeal to alignment)
- Normalizing (Managing this kind of conflict is just part of doing the job)
- Playing to one's own strengths (if better at writing than speaking, develop a memo)

*Organizational context*

- Explicit organizational policies, values
- Organizational value placed on open debate, discussion
- Existing explicit mechanisms for open debate and discussion within the organization (e.g., town meetings)
- Systems for raising questions (e.g., hotline, ombudsman)
- Consistent and visible organizational track record of values-based leadership and practice and of correcting problems

### D. Personal-Professional Profile

**In your definition of a well-run company, how important are the following?**

*Please indicate whether each quality is "very important," "somewhat important," or "not important at all."*

a. Provides excellent customer service
   Very important   Somewhat important   Not important at all

b. Has efficient and flexible operations
   Very important   Somewhat important   Not important at all

c. Offers high financial return to shareholders
   Very important   Somewhat important   Not important at all

d. Attracts and retains exceptional people
   Very important   Somewhat important   Not important at all

e. Creates products or services that benefit society
   Very important   Somewhat important   Not important at all

f. Adheres to a strong mission
   Very important   Somewhat important   Not important at all

g. Invests in employee training and professional development
   Very important   Somewhat important   Not important at all

h. Operates according to its values and a strong code of ethics
   Very important   Somewhat important   Not important at all

i. Is a stable employer
   Very important   Somewhat important   Not important at all

j. Provides competitive compensation
   Very important   Somewhat important   Not important at all

k. Adheres to progressive environmental policies
   Very important   Somewhat important   Not important at all

l. Produces high-quality products and services
   Very important   Somewhat important   Not important at all

*Would you add something to the previous list that you think is "very important"? If so, what?*

## Which of the following issues pose the greatest challenges for today's CEOs and senior executives?

*Please choose a maximum of three alternatives.*

_____ Lack of investor confidence

_____ Increased activism on the part of environmental and social advocacy groups

_____ Corporate scandal (e.g., accounting misstatements, conflict of interest)

_____ Questions about executive compensation levels and incentive systems

_____ Breakdown in trust between employees and management

_____ Inadequate regulatory and legal institutions

_____ Product safety and liability

_____ Economic downturn

_____ Growing inequity in the distribution of wealth around the world

_____ Lack of public trust in business

_____ Managing international supply chain requirements

_____ War and international instability

_____ Threat of terrorism

_____ Other (please specify) _____

**To what extent do you agree or disagree with the following statements?**

*Please indicate whether you "strongly agree," "somewhat agree," "somewhat disagree," or "strongly disagree" with each.*

a. Businesspeople are more likely to care about the social responsibilities of companies when the economy is strong.

Strongly agree    Somewhat agree    Somewhat disagree    Strongly disagree

b. When a multinational company is entering a new market in a less-developed country, it has a responsibility to go above and beyond business success and contribute to the development of the local community.

Strongly agree    Somewhat agree    Somewhat disagree    Strongly disagree

c. When it comes to the environment, all a company needs to do is comply with the law.

Strongly agree    Somewhat agree    Somewhat disagree    Strongly disagree

d. Companies should maintain their employees' job security even if they incur a short-term drop in profit as a result.

Strongly agree    Somewhat agree    Somewhat disagree    Strongly disagree

e. Most companies accurately report their earnings and profits.

Strongly agree    Somewhat agree    Somewhat disagree    Strongly disagree

f. Corporate reputation is important to me in making my decision about the organization where I want to work.

Strongly agree    Somewhat agree    Somewhat disagree    Strongly disagree

g. Managers place too much emphasis on short-term performance measures when making business decisions.

Strongly agree    Somewhat agree    Somewhat disagree    Strongly disagree

h. I anticipate that my own values will sometimes conflict with what I am asked to do in business.

Strongly agree    Somewhat agree    Somewhat disagree    Strongly disagree

*If you answered the last statement above with "somewhat agree" or "strongly agree," please specify which kinds of values conflicts you expect to face.*

**Assume you are engaged in each of the following business activities or practices. How likely do you think it is that values conflicts would arise?**

*Please indicate whether it is "very likely," "somewhat likely," or "not likely at all" that values conflicts would arise.*

a. Managing personnel in manufacturing plants
   Very likely     Somewhat likely     Not likely at all

b. Outsourcing production operations
   Very likely     Somewhat likely     Not likely at all

c. Investing in less-developed countries
   Very likely     Somewhat likely     Not likely at all

d. Downsizing
   Very likely     Somewhat likely     Not likely at all

e. Financial reporting
   Very likely     Somewhat likely     Not likely at all

f. Natural resource exploration
   Very likely     Somewhat likely     Not likely at all

g. Awarding stock options
   Very likely     Somewhat likely     Not likely at all

h. Setting executive compensation levels
   Very likely     Somewhat likely     Not likely at all

i. Conducting performance reviews
   Very likely     Somewhat likely     Not likely at all

j. Interacting with government officials
   Very likely     Somewhat likely     Not likely at all

k. Raising or borrowing capital
   Very likely     Somewhat likely     Not likely at all

l. Negotiating with suppliers or customers
   Very likely     Somewhat likely     Not likely at all

**If you find that your values conflict with those of the company where you work, how likely is it that you will:**

a. Not mind too much

    Very likely      Somewhat likely      Not likely at all

b. Experience it as stressful

    Very likely      Somewhat likely      Not likely at all

c. Quietly handle the stress

    Very likely      Somewhat likely      Not likely at all

d. Look for another job

    Very likely      Somewhat likely      Not likely at all

e. Speak up about your objections

    Very likely      Somewhat likely      Not likely at all

f. Advocate alternative values or approaches within the company

    Very likely      Somewhat likely      Not likely at all

g. Try to get others to join you in addressing your concerns

    Very likely      Somewhat likely      Not likely at all

**Think of a few occasions when you encountered a values conflict in your previous work experience. Recall how you handled the situations. Would you characterize yourself and your behavior as that of:**

\_\_\_\_\_ *an idealist* (One who is primarily concerned with moral ideals when making decisions on how to act.)

\_\_\_\_\_ *a pragmatist* (One who is concerned with his or her own material welfare, but also with moral ideals. "Pragmatists will gladly do their fair share to create a civil society, but not place themselves at a systematic disadvantage" to do so.)

\_\_\_\_\_ *an opportunist* (One who is only concerned with his or her own material welfare.)

*If you placed yourself in the category of "pragmatist," what can you do to maximize the likelihood that you will act on your ideals? What competencies will you need?*

**Think of someone you deeply respect. What are the 2 or 3 characteristics you most admire in this person?**

**Who are you at your best?**

**Name your 3 or 4 deepest values.**

**What is the one sentence you would like to see in your obituary that captures who you really were in your life?**

## Questions of Personal Purpose

*What is your personal purpose for your business career? Some possible issues to consider:*

- What impact do you want to have? On whom?
- Whom do you want to know you benefited? In what ways?
- What do you want to learn?
- How do you define your impact as an auditor, investor, manager, product developer, marketer, senior executive, and so on?
- What do you hope to accomplish? What will make your professional life worthwhile?
- How do you want to feel about yourself and your work, both while you are doing it and in the end?

## Questions of Risk

- Are you a risk taker or risk averse?
- What are the greatest risks you face in your line of work? Are they personal (e.g., livelihood, deportation, legal punishment) or are they professional (e.g., harm to customers, employees, the firm), or are they societal (e.g., impact on environment, profession, industry, nation)?
- What levels of risk can and can't you live with?

## Questions of Personal Communication Style or Preference

- Do you deal well with conflict or are you nonconfrontational? Under what circumstances do you behave in each way?
- Do you prefer communicating in person or in writing?
- Do you think best from the gut and in the moment or do you need to take time to reflect and craft your communications?
- Do you assert your position with statements or do you use questions to communicate?

## Questions of Loyalty

- Do you tend to feel the greatest loyalty to family, work colleagues, your firm or employer, or other stakeholders, such as customers?
- Under what conditions and given what stakes?

## Questions of Self-Image

- Do you see yourself as shrewd or naive?
- As idealistic, opportunistic, or pragmatic?
- As a learner or as a teacher?
- Other?

*Note:* The first 14 questions in this profile were piloted at the University of Texas, Austin, in 2003. Questions 1 and 3–7 are used with permission from the Aspen Institute Business and Society Program MBA Student Attitudes Surveys {{www.aspencbe.org}}. Questions 10–14 are adapted from Jim Loehr and Tony Schwartz, *The Power of Full Engagement: Managing Energy, Not Time, Is the Key to High Performance and Personal Renewal* (New York: Free Press, 2003). Questions 15–19 are based on the Giving Voice to Values interview findings.

The self-assessment here is only lightly focused on values clarification. This is because, as discussed in Chapter 2, most assessments of true core moral values tend to generate a similar short list of values. Rather the focus here is on an individualized assessment of personal strengths, communication style, and so on.

Idealist," "pragmatist," and "opportunist" categories and descriptions are drawn from Gregory Dees and Peter Crampton, "Shrewd Bargaining on the Moral Frontier: Toward a Theory of Morality in Practice," *Business Ethics Quarterly,* vol. 1, no. 2 (April 1991): 135–167.

## E.  Guidelines for Peer Coaching

*Insightful and supportive peer feedback on discussants' proposed "scripts" and strategies for responding to values conflicts is an essential part of the Giving Voice to Values approach. This does not mean that there is no critique. Rather it means that those who share their proposed responses to the values conflict, as well as those who are serving as peer coaches, all adopt a stance of joint problem-solving. This includes noting the strengths of a proposed response (so that they can be retained) as well as identifying the remaining questions (so that the group can collaborate on more effective solutions). What follows is a template for listening to and debriefing the sharing of proposed "scripts" and strategies for responding to values conflicts.*

### Preliminary Reflection

*Directed to Listeners*

After listening to your colleague's response to the values conflict under discussion but before discussing it, take a moment to silently consider your responses to the following questions.

- What is your immediate response to your colleague's strategy and "script"?
- What are the strengths of this response?
- What questions do you still have for your colleague?
- If you were the target of this response, how do you think you would react?
- What might improve this response?

*Directed to Speakers*

After sharing your response to the values conflict under discussion but before discussing it, take a moment to silently consider your responses to the following questions.

- What do you see as the strengths of your response?
- What still concerns you?
- What do you think would be helpful in enabling you to respond more effectively? What would you like to ask for from your peers?

**Process Questions**
- Invite speakers to share their answers to the questions above.
- Invite listeners to share their answers to the questions above.
- Invite speakers to respond to the following: Is that a helpful response to you?
- If yes, why?
- If no, why not? What would be more helpful?

*When designing, reflecting upon, and discussing responses to values conflicts, the following questions may be useful:*

- Who is the critical audience(s)? What is at stake for them?
- What is the optimal timing for your effort? Should it be broken down into stages in some way? Sequenced?
- Will you do this solo? With allies? (If yes, whom?)
- Will you do this off-line or in public? One-on-one or in a group?
- Do you have all the information you need (research, interpersonal insights, examples of past successes or failures, etc.)?
- Do you have adequate sources of support, inside or outside the organization? You might brainstorm all the possible sources of support and what you think each of them may be best able to provide. For example:
Peers within the organization may have information and be able to confirm or disprove your data.
Family members may be able to place the choice into a larger perspective, with regard to your deepest values and your personal identity. It may also be helpful to discuss your situation with family members as a way of engaging them in the process

*with* you so that you are not on this journey alone, particularly when the risks may affect them as well. Otherwise, fear of admitting the risks to those close to us can hinder our sense of free decision making.

- Given your own self-assessment of your typical reactions and blindspots, have you insured that you have consulted advisers who are best suited to raise what you are likely to miss?

*How would you describe the approach you take in your proposed response:*

*A learning stance:* Open-minded (e.g., "Help me to understand your thinking about this...")

*Dialogue* (e.g., "Can we keep this decision open for a while longer, so that we can consider other perspectives?")

*Persuasion:* You are convinced of your position but want to persuade the other (e.g., "I have done a lot of thinking about this situation and I have concluded . . . I would really appreciate the opportunity to share my perspective with you").

*Adversarial:* You are convinced of your position and your goal is to simply state your position and let the chips fall where they may (e.g., "I have done a lot of thinking about this situation and I have concluded . . . I am sorry if you disagree but I cannot pursue this course of action").

*One-size-fits-all arguments, or somehow tailored for audience(s)* ("It's not honest" is a one-size-fits-all argument. A more tailored argument might be: "Our firm's reputation for honesty is its greatest asset. Remember how our customers stood by us when we discovered that data theft last year? That was because they believed we would never deceive them about their risks." Both can be effective in different situations, but it is best to be aware of our choices.)

*Problem-solving* (e.g., "I see what's at stake here and why you are suggesting this course of action, but I am confident we can find another solution if we bring all our talents to bear here.")

*Other approaches?*

- What is the biggest challenge or thorniest argument you face?
- What are your strongest arguments?
- What will it take to *do* this?
- For your target audience: How will you need to frame this choice to tap into your audience's commitment?
- For yourself: How will you need to frame this choice to tap into your own commitment and courage?

### F. An Action Framework for Giving Voice to Values: The To-Do List

1. **Values**

   Know and appeal to a short list of widely shared values, such as honesty, respect, responsibility, fairness, and compassion.*
   In other words, don't assume too little—or too much—commonality with the viewpoints of others.

2. **Choice**

   Discover and believe you have a choice about voicing values by examining your own track record. Know what has enabled and disabled you in the past, so you can work with and around these factors. And recognize, respect, and appeal to the capacity for choice in others.

3. **Normality**

   Expect values conflicts so that you approach them calmly and competently. Overreaction can limit your choices unnecessarily.

4. **Purpose**

   Define your personal and professional purpose explicitly and broadly before values conflicts arise: What is the impact you most want to have in your work, profession, and career? Similarly, appeal to a sense of purpose in others.

5. **Self-Knowledge, Self-Image, and Alignment**

   Generate a "self-story" or personal narrative about the decision to voice and act on your values that is consistent with who you already are and builds on the strengths and preferences that you already recognize in yourself. There are many ways to align your unique strengths and style with your values. If you view yourself as a "pragmatist," for example, find a way to view voicing your values as pragmatic.

## 6. Voice

Voice is developed over time and with practice. Practice voicing your values using the style of expression with which you are most skillful and which is most appropriate to the situation. You are most likely to say those words that you have pre-scripted and already heard yourself express, at earlier times in your career or in practice sessions.

## 7. Reasons and Rationalizations

Anticipate the typical rationalizations given for ethically questionable behavior and identify counterarguments. These rationalizations are predictable and vulnerable to reasoned response.

*Rushworth M. Kidder, *Moral Courage: Taking Action When Your Values Are Put to the Test* (New York: William Morrow, 2005).

# Notes

INTRODUCTION

1. David M. Messick and Max H. Bazerman, "Ethical Leadership and the Psychology of Decision-Making," *Sloan Management Review,* vol. 37, no. 2 (Winter 1996): 9–22.

2. Ethics Resource Center, "2007 National Business Ethics Survey: An Inside View of Private Sector Ethics," *Ethics Resource Center,* 2007, <www.ethics.org/files/u5/The_2007_National_Business_Ethics_Survey.pdf> (2 September 2009).

3. And once we have tried to raise issues internally, if unsuccessful, we may feel the need to take more public action.

4. Robert Kane, *Through the Moral Maze: Searching for Absolute Values in a Pluralistic World* (Armonk: M.E. Sharpe, 1996), 10.

5. Much of this section is drawn from Mary C. Gentile, "Is There Free Will in Business? Leadership and Social Impact Management," in *Handbook of Responsible Leadership and Governance in Global Business,* ed. Jonathan P. Doh and Stephen A. Stumpf (Northampton, Mass.: Edward Elgar, 2005).

6. The surveys were conducted by the Aspen Institute's Center for Business Education, part of the Business and Society Program. Student responses to the surveys (*Where Will They Lead: MBA Student Attitudes About Business and Society*) can be found at <www.aspenCBE.org> (25 January 2009).

7. Although the essays I read happened to be from Columbia (I was engaged as a consultant at the time, assisting with their ethics curriculum development), the types of stories the students shared are very similar to stories I have heard from business students and business practitioners across many settings.

8. Perry London, "The Rescuers: Motivational Hypotheses About

Christians Who Saved Jews from the Nazis," in *Altruism and Help-ing Behavior: Social Psychological Studies of Some Antecedents and Consequences,* ed. Jacqueline R. Macaulay and Leonard Berkowitz (New York: Academic, 1970), 241–250; Douglas H. Huneke, *The Moses of Rovno* (New York: Dodd, Mead, 1985).

9. Unless otherwise specified, the case examples in this collection were inspired by interviews and observations of actual experi-ences, but names and other situational details have been changed for confidentiality and teaching purposes.

# 1
## GIVING VOICE TO OUR VALUES

1. Barbara L. Fredrickson, *Positivity* (New York: Crown, 2009).

# 2
## VALUES

1. Rushworth M. Kidder, *Moral Courage: Taking Action When Your Values Are Put to the Test* (New York: William Morrow, 2005), 39–76.

2. Martin E. P. Seligman, *Authentic Happiness: Using the New Positive Psychology to Realize Your Potential for Lasting Fulfillment* (New York: Simon and Schuster, 2002).

3. See <www.viastrengths.org/index.aspx?ContentID=44>.

4. Kidder, *Moral Courage,* 47.

5. Thomas Donaldson and Thomas W. Dunfee, *Ties That Bind: A Social Contracts Approach to Business Ethics* (Boston: Harvard Business School Press, 1999), 43–44.

6. Mary C. Gentile, "Ways of Thinking About and Across Differ-ences." *Harvard Business School* (January 1995): Case no. 486083-HCB-ENG. This note includes a definitional model for diversity

that provides more common ground for speaking about values across different identities.

7. Research into empowerment, control systems, dissent, organizational loyalty, pay for performance, organizational learning, teamwork, diversity, and many other topics illustrates powerful influence and socialization impacts that organizations can have, for good and ill. Examples appear in subsequent chapters, and the bibliography includes references.

8. Available at <www.GivingVoiceToValues.org>.

9. This exercise is known as "A Tale of Two Stories," a foundational activity in the GVV approach that is discussed in greater detail in Chapter 3.

10. The full results from these student attitude surveys can be obtained at <www.aspenCBE.org>.

11. Psychologist Daniel Gilbert explains that human beings tend to respond more readily to threats that are perceived as personal and intentional, disgusting, or immoral (the examples are tangible and visceral—having to do with sex or flag-burning—as opposed to the more cerebral questions of the morality of earnings management), imminent and instantaneous (rather than gradual). This is not to say that longer-term and more general threats cannot be perceived, but rather that they require a more deliberate and practiced approach. See Nicholas D. Kristof, "When Our Brains Short-Circuit," *New York Times*, 1 July 2009.

## 3
### A TALE OF TWO STORIES

1. This assumption is discussed in more detail in Chapter 6, under "idealists," "pragmatists," and "opportunists."

2. In this exercise, a "values conflict" refers to a disagreement that has an ethical or moral dimension to it. Disagreeing over an idea about the most efficient process flow design for an assembly line

most likely reflects a difference in analytic approach or assumptions, but there is usually not an ethical component. If one design reflected a commitment to worker safety or environmental concerns, however, and the other did not, this disagreement might be appropriate here.

3. This alignment of personal strengths and approach is discussed in Chapter 6.

4. This is a familiar tool commonly shared in business ethics texts and seminars, counseling individuals who are faced with ethical dilemmas to "think about how you would feel if your decision appeared on the front page of *The Wall Street Journal*," or, my favorite variation, if your mother heard about it.

5. Mary C. Gentile and William Klepper, with the assistance of Clelia Peters and Miguel Lopez, "'This Whole System Seems Wrong': Felipe Montez and Concerns About the Global Supply Chain," *Giving Voice to Values* collection, <www.GivingVoiceTo Values.org>, and Columbia CaseWorks, no. 081803, <www4.gsb .columbia.edu/caseworks>.

6. Mary C. Gentile, "Is This My Place? (A) and (B)," *Giving Voice to Values* collection, <www.GivingVoiceToValues.org>.

7. Mary C. Gentile, "The Independent Director's Challenge (A) and (B)," *Giving Voice to Values* collection, <www.GivingVoiceTo Values.org>.

8. Mary C. Gentile and William Klepper, with the assistance of Sharon Sarosky and Suprita Goyal, "The Client Who Fell Through the Cracks (A) and (B)," *Giving Voice to Values* collection, <www.GivingVoiceToValues.org>, and Columbia Case-Works, no. 081801, <www4.gsb.columbia.edu/caseworks>.

9. Gentile and Klepper, "'This Whole System Seems Wrong.'"

10. The story of the diversity consultant in Chapter 6 is a vivid example of this debunking of a previously unquestioned assumption.

11. Jonathan Haidt, *The Happiness Hypothesis: Finding Modern Truth in Ancient Wisdom* (New York: Basic, 2006), 102.

## 4
### IT'S ONLY NORMAL

1. These ideas and this quotation are from Judith Samuelson and Mary Gentile, "Get Aggressive About Passivity," *Harvard Business Review* (November 2005): 18–20.

2. Linda Hill and Suzy Wetlaufer, "Leadership When There Is No One to Ask: An Interview with Eni's Franco Bernabe," *Harvard Business Review* (July–August 1998): 81–94.

3. Mary Gentile, under the supervision of Todd D. Jick, "Donna Dubinksy and Apple Computer, Inc. (A)," *Harvard Business School*, 1986, Case no. 395117-PDF-ENG.

4. Haidt, *Happiness Hypothesis*, 74. This kind of "self-serving bias" has been researched by others, such as James Friedrich, "On Seeing One-Self as Less Self-Serving than Others: The Ultimate Self-Serving Bias," *Teaching of Psychology*, vol. 23 (1996): 107–109, and Anne Tenbrunsel and David Messick, "Ethical Fading: The Role of Self-Deception in Unethical Behavior," *Social Justice Research*, vol. 17, no. 2 (June 2004): 223–236.

5. Mary C. Gentile, "Be Careful What You Wish For: From the Middle," *Giving Voice to Values* collection, <www.GivingVoiceToValues.org>.

6. The tensions and contradictions managers face regarding financial reporting are discussed further in Chapter 5.

7. Ahmed Belkaoui, *The Coming Crisis in Accounting* (New York: Quorum, 1989), 63.

## 5
### WHAT AM I WORKING FOR?

1. James Collins and Jerry Porras, *Built to Last: Successful Habits of Visionary Companies* (New York: HarperCollins, 1994), 91.

2. Courses on "social entrepreneurship" increased nearly 500 per-

cent between 2003 and 2009; see <www.BeyondGreyPinstripes
.org>. According to the Aspen Institute Student Attitude Survey,
when MBA students were asked to prioritize factors in their job
search: "In the 2007 survey, 25.8% of students chose 'potential to
make a contribution to society' as a priority, compared with only
15.3% in 2002" (April 2008). Aspen Institute Center for Business
Education, *Where Will They Lead? 2008 MBA Student Attitudes
About Business and Society* (Full Research Report), 28.

3. Charles Handy, "What's a Business For?" *Harvard Business Review* (December 2002): 49–55.

4. Robert H. Frank, *What Price the Moral High Ground? Ethical Dilemmas in Competitive Environments* (Princeton: Princeton University Press, 2004), 13.

5. Joel Brockner, "Why It's So Hard to Be Fair," *Harvard Business Review* (March 2006): 122–129.

6. Mary C. Gentile, "A Personal Struggle with the Definition of Success," *Giving Voice to Values* collection, <www.GivingVoiceTo Values.org>.

7. This discussion is based on observations of graduate financial and managerial accounting classes, discussions with accounting scholars, and interviews and written accounts from both managers and MBA students about their work experience prior to matriculation. Much of this thinking is more fully discussed in Mary C. Gentile, "Discussions About Ethics in the Accounting Classroom: Student Assumptions and Faculty Paradigms," *Giving Voice to Values* collection, <www.GivingVoiceToValues.org>.

# 6
## PLAYING TO MY STRENGTHS

1. Kidder, *Moral Courage,* 82.

2. Gregory Dees and Peter Crampton, "Shrewd Bargaining on the

Moral Frontier: Toward a Theory of Morality in Practice," *Business Ethics Quarterly*, vol. 1, no. 2 (April 1991): 135–167.

3. See, for example, Uri Gneezy, "Deception: The Role of Consequences," *The American Economic Review*, vol. 95, no. 1 (March 2005): 384–394.

4. For more on the conscious use of narrative in our careers, see Herminia Ibarra, "What's Your Story?" *Harvard Business Review*, vol. 83, no. 1 (January 2005): 64–71; Herminia Ibarra, "Provisional Selves: Experimenting with Image and Identity in Professional Adaptation," *Administrative Science Quarterly*, vol. 44, no. 4 (December 1999): 764–791.

5. Mary C. Gentile, "The Diversity Consultant (A) and (B)," *Giving Voice to Values* collection, <www.GivingVoiceToValues.org>.

6. Mary C. Gentile, "Naïveté or Boldness (A) and (B)," *Giving Voice to Values* collection, <www.GivingVoiceToValues.org>.

7. These ideas are discussed in more depth in Chapter 8.

8. Robert Prentice, "Teaching Ethics, Heuristics, and Biases," *Journal of Business Ethics Education*, vol. 1, no. 1 (2004): 57–74.

9. Irving L. Janis, "Groupthink," *Psychology Today*, vol. 5, no. 6 (November 1971): 43–76.

10. Mary Catherine Bateson, *Willing to Learn: Passages of Personal Discovery* (Hanover, N.H.: Steerforth, 2004), 66–76.

11. Bateson, *Willing to Learn*, 68.

# 7
## FINDING MY VOICE

1. There are numerous studies on these phenomena, including the work of Teresa Amabile, Max Bazerman, Joel Brockner, Amy Edmondson, Robert Frank, Irving Janis, Joshua Margolis, David Messick, Frances Milliken, Elizabeth Morrison, and Ann Tenbrunsel.

2. Laura Landro, "Bring Surgeons Down to Earth: New Programs Aim to Curb Fear That Prevents Nurses from Flagging Problems," *Wall Street Journal,* 16 November 2005.

3. For example, M. H. Bazerman, G. Loewenstein, and D. A. Moore, "Why Good Accountants Do Bad Audits," *Harvard Business Review* (November 2002): 96–102.

4. Amy C. Edmondson, "Speaking Up in the Operating Room: How Team Leaders Promote Learning in Interdisciplinary Action Teams," *Journal of Management Studies,* vol. 40, no. 6 (September 2003): 1419–1452.

5. Elizabeth Morrison and Frances J. Milliken, "Organizational Silence: A Barrier to Change and Development in a Pluralistic World," *Academy of Management Review,* vol. 25, no. 4 (2000): 706–725.

6. Mary C. Gentile and William Klepper, with the assistance of Sharon Sarosky and Suprita Goyal, "The Client Who Fell Through the Cracks (A) and (B)," *Giving Voice to Values* collection, <www.GivingVoiceToValues.org>, and Columbia CaseWorks, no. 081801, <www4.gsb.columbia.edu/caseworks>.

7. Brockner, "Why It's So Hard to Be Fair," 7–8.

8. Jerry Goodstein and Mary C. Gentile, "Better Wrong Than Right? Delivering the 'Bad' Market Research News (A) and (B)," *Giving Voice To Values* collection, <www.GivingVoiceToValues.org>.

9. Mary C. Gentile, "Lisa Baxter: Developing a Voice," *Giving Voice to Values* collection, <www.GivingVoiceToValues.org>.

10. Haidt, *Happiness Hypothesis,* 145–149.

11. See, for example, Kathy Kram, *Mentoring at Work* (Lanham, Md.: University Press of America, 1988); Kathy Kram and Belle Rose Ragins, *Handbook of Mentoring at Work: Theory, Research, and Practice* (Thousand Oaks, Calif.: Sage, 2007); David Thomas, John J. Gabarro, and Don Tapscott, *Breaking Through: The Making of Minority Executives in Corporate America* (Boston: Harvard Business School Press, 1999).

12. Stanley Milgram's experiments at Yale in the 1960s are a striking and disquieting illustration of the degree to which people are able and even inclined to defer to presumed expertise and authority; more recent and actual experiences (as opposed to experimental simulation) at Abu Ghraib are a sobering reminder of this reality.

13. See the case studies: Mary C. Gentile, "Jeff Salett ... From the Top, Sort of (A) and (B)," and "Is This My Place? ... Speaking 'Up' (A) and (B)," *Giving Voice to Values* collection, <www.GivingVoice ToValues.org>.

# 8
## REASONS AND RATIONALIZATIONS

1. Haidt, *Happiness Hypothesis,* 145–149.
2. Dees and Crampton, "Shrewd Bargaining on the Moral Frontier," 146, 164.
3. Kidder, *Moral Courage,* 89.
4. It is useful to distinguish the value of "loyalty" from the personal predilection to feel a greater sense of loyalty in one area or another of one's life, as discussed in the self-assessment discussion in Chapter 6. In Chapter 6, we were working to recognize our own predispositions or unthinking tendencies, such that we could play to them when trying to make it easier to voice our values. For example, if I tend to be driven by a commitment to my work team, then framing my values conflict so it is about protecting and serving my team will make it feel more natural to me.
5. John G. Simon, Charles W. Powers, and Jon P. Gunnemann, *The Ethical Investor: Universities and Corporate Responsibility* (New Haven: Yale University Press, 1972), 22–25.
6. Mary C. Gentile, "Reasons and Rationalization," *GivingVoice to Values* collection, <www.GivingVoiceToValues.org>.

7. Prentice, "Teaching Ethics," 57–74. Prentice also refers readers to a self-assessment survey that can be used to reveal our own decision biases, in Scott Plous, *The Psychology of Judgment and Decision-Making* (New York: McGraw-Hill, 1993), 1–12. Other resources on this topic include Messick and Bazerman, "Ethical Leadership," 9–22; Mary C. Gentile, "Ways of Thinking About and Across Differences," *Harvard Business School* (January 1995), Case no. 395–117; Thomas Gilovich, *How We Know What Isn't So: The Fallibility of Human Reason in Everyday Life* (New York: Free Press, 1991); Howard Gardner, *Changing Minds: The Art and Science of Changing Our Own and Other People's Minds* (Boston: Harvard Business School Press, 2006); Minette E. Drumwright and Patrick E. Murphy, "How Advertising Practitioners View Ethics: Moral Muteness, Moral Myopia, and Moral Imagination," *Journal of Advertising,* vol. 33, no. 2 (Summer 2004): 7–24.

8. Janis, "Groupthink," 43–76.

9. Francis Flynn and Jennifer A. Chatman, "What's the Norm Here? Social Categorization as a Basis for Group Norm Development," in *Research on Managing Groups and Teams,* vol. 5 (2002), ed. E. Mannix and M. Neale, 135–160.

10. Prentice, "Teaching Ethics," 64.

11. Karl E. Weick, "Small Wins: Redefining the Scale of Social Problems," *American Psychologist* (January 1984): 40–49.

12. Prentice, "Teaching Ethics," 68.

13. Chris Argyris, "Teaching Smart People How to Learn," *Harvard Business Review* (May–June 1991): 103.

14. Prentice, "Teaching Ethics," 67.

15. Prentice, "Teaching Ethics," 67. Messick and Bazerman, "Ethical Leadership," 9–22, makes a similar argument, explaining that when confronted with the complexity of decision making, people often oversimplify in order to find a way to act. Like Karl Weick, they observe our tendency to become overwhelmed but rather than naturally pursuing the strategic redefinition of large prob-

lems that Weick recommends, we often fall prey to a set of decision biases (similar to those Prentice pointed out but labeled differently): Ignoring low-probability events; Limiting the search
for stakeholders; Ignoring the possibility that the public will "find
out"; Discounting the future; and Undervaluing collective outcomes (e.g., Externalities).
16. Gardner, *Changing Minds,* 66.

# 9
## PUTTING IT TO WORK

1. Albert O. Hirschman, *Exit, Voice, and Loyalty: Responses to Decline in Firms, Organizations, and States* (Cambridge: Harvard
   University Press, 1970).
2. Based on Ranjini Swamy and Swapnil Naik, "The Temple En-
   croachment Issue (A) and (B)," *Giving Voice to Values* collection,
   <www.GivingVoiceToValues.org>.
3. Andrew Molinsky and Joshua Margolis, "Necessary Evils and Interpersonal Sensitivity in Organizations," *Academy of Management Review,* vol. 30 (2005): 245–268.
4. Teresa M. Amabile, Constance N. Hadley, and Steven J. Kramer,
   "Creativity Under the Gun," *Harvard Business Review* (August
   2002): 52–61.
5. The "time outs" and "safety pauses" discussed in Chapter 7 are
   also useful in this context.
6. Thank you to Karen From for this powerful example.
7. Mary C. Gentile, Gary E. Jusela, and William Wiggenhorn, "Raising the Stakes or Finally Seeing Them Clearly? Balanced Leadership in Time of Economic Crisis," *New Academy Review,* vol. 1,
   no. 1 (February 2002): 37–47.

# Bibliography

Allen, William T. "Our Schizophrenic Conception of the Business Corporation." *Cardozo Law Review,* vol. 14, no. 261 (1992–1993): 261–281.

Altucher, James. "Candor Counts When Keeping Investors Calm." *Financial Times,* 28 March 2005, 21.

Amabile, Teresa M., Constance N. Hadley, and Steven J. Kramer. "Creativity Under the Gun." *Harvard Business Review* (August 2002): 52–61.

Argyris, Chris. "Teaching Smart People How to Learn." *Harvard Business Review* (May-June 1991): 103.

Ayres, Ian, and Barry Nalebuff. "In Praise of Honest Pricing." *MIT Sloan Management Review* (Fall 2003): 24–28.

Badaracco, Joseph. *Defining Moments: When Managers Must Choose Between Right and Right.* Boston: Harvard Business School Press, 1997.

Bagley, Constance E. *Winning Legally: How to Use the Law to Create Value, Marshal Resources, and Manage Risk.* Boston: Harvard Business School Press, 2005.

Bateson, Mary Catherine. *Willing to Learn: Passages of Personal Discovery.* Hanover, N.H.: Steerforth, 2004.

Bazerman, M. H., G. Loewenstein, and D. A. Moore. "Why Good Accountants Do Bad Audits." *Harvard Business Review* (November 2002): 96–102.

Belkaoui, Ahmed. *The Coming Crisis in Accounting.* New York: Quorum, 1989.

Bird, Frederick Bruce. *The Muted Conscience: Moral Silence and the Practice of Ethics in Business.* Westport, Conn.: Quorum, 1996.

Bird, Frederick B., and James A. Waters. "The Moral Muteness of Managers." *California Management Review* (Fall 1989): 73–88.

Blair, Margaret. "Reforming Corporate Governance: What History Can Teach Us." *Berkeley Business Law Journal,* vol. 1, no. 1 (Spring 2004): 1–44.

Bower, Joseph, and Stuart Gilson. "Forethought Thinking About . . . The

Social Cost of Fraud and Bankruptcy." *Harvard Business Review* (December 2003): 20–22.

Brockner, Joel. "Why It's So Hard to Be Fair." *Harvard Business Review* (March 2006): 122–129.

Cialdini, Robert B. *Influence: Science and Practice.* Boston: Allyn and Bacon, 2001.

Cialdini, Robert B., Petia K. Petrova, and Noah J. Goldstein. "The Hidden Costs of Organizational Dishonesty." *MIT Sloan Management Review,* vol. 45, no. 3 (Spring 2004): 67–73.

Collins, James, and Jerry Porras. *Built to Last: Successful Habits of Visionary Companies.* New York: HarperCollins, 1994.

Cragg, Wesley. "Teaching Business Ethics: The Role of Ethics in Business and in Business Education." *Journal of Business Ethics,* issue 16 (1997): 231–245.

Creed, W. E. Douglas. "Voice Lessons: Tempered Radicalism and the Use of Voice and Silence." *The Journal of Management Studies* (Fall 2003): 1503–1536.

Cross, Robert L., and Susan E. Brodt. "How Assumptions of Consensus Undermine Decision Making." *MIT Sloan Management Review,* vol. 42, no. 2 (Winter 2001): 86–94.

Davis, Ian. "How to Escape the Short-Term Trap." *The McKinsey Quarterly,* April 2005, <www.mckinseyquarterly.com/article_print.aspx?L2 =21&L3=34&ar=1611>.

Dees, Gregory, and Peter Crampton. "Shrewd Bargaining on the Moral Frontier: Toward a Theory of Morality in Practice." *Business Ethics Quarterly,* vol. 1, no. 2 (April 1991): 135–167.

Diener, Ed, and Martin E. P. Seligman. "Beyond Money: Toward an Economy of Well-Being." *Psychological Science in the Public Interest,* vol. 5, no. 1 (2001): 1–31.

Doh, Jonathan P., and Stephen A. Stumpf, eds. *Handbook of Responsible Leadership and Governance in Global Business.* Northampton, Mass.: Edward Elgar, 2005.

Donaldson, Thomas, and Thomas W. Dunfee. *Ties That Bind: A Social Contracts Approach to Business Ethics.* Boston: Harvard Business School Press, 1999.

Drumwright, Minette E., and Patrick E. Murphy. "How Advertising Prac-

titioners View Ethics: Moral Muteness, Moral Myopia, and Moral Imagination." *Journal of Advertising,* vol. 33, no. 2 (Summer 2004): 7–24.

Edmonson, Amy C. "Speaking Up in the Operating Room: How Team
Leaders Promote Learning in Interdisciplinary Action Teams." *Journal
of Management Studies,* vol. 40, no. 6 (September 2003): 1419–1452.

El Saadawi, Nawal. *Death of an Ex-Minister,* translated by Shirley Eber.
London: Minerva Paperback by Mandarin Paperbacks, 1992.

Ethics Resource Center. "2007 National Business Ethics Survey: An Inside View of Private Sector Ethics." *Ethics Resource Center.* 2007. <www.
ethics.org/files/u5/The_2007_National_Business_Ethics_
Survey.pdf> (2 September 2009).

Fehr, Ernst, and Urs Fischbacher. "The Nature of Human Altruism." *Nature,* vol. 4225 (23 October 2003): 785–791.

Flynn, Francis, and Jennifer A. Chatman. "What's the Norm Here? Social
Categorization as a Basis for Group Norm Development." In *Research
on Managing Groups and Teams,* vol. 5 (2002), ed. E. Mannix and
M. Neale, pp. 135–160.

Frank, Robert H. *What Price the Moral High Ground? Ethical Dilemmas
in Competitive Environments.* Princeton: Princeton University Press,
2004.

Frank, Robert H. "Economic Scene." *New York Times.* 17 February 2005.

Fredrickson, Barbara L. *Positivity.* New York: Crown, 2009.

Friedman, Stewart D., Perry Christensen, and Jessica DeGroot. "Work
and Life: The End of the Zero-Sum Game." *Harvard Business Review*
(November-December 1998): 119–129.

Friedrich, James. "On Seeing One-Self as Less Self-Serving than Others:
The Ultimate Self-Serving Bias." *Teaching of Psychology,* vol. 23 (1996):
107–109.

Fuller, Joseph, and Michael C. Jensen. "Just Say No to Wall Street: Putting
a Stop to the Earnings Game." *Journal of Applied Corporate Finance,*
vol. 14, no. 4 (Winter 2002): 41–46.

Gardner, Howard. *Changing Minds: The Art and Science of Changing Our
Own and Other People's Minds.* Boston: Harvard Business School
Press, 2006.

Gentile, Mary C. "Ways of Thinking About and Across Differences." *Harvard Business School* (January 1995): Case no. 486083-HCB-ENG.

Gentile, Mary C. "The 21st Century MBA." *Strategy+Business,* issue 51 (Summer 2008): 88–91.

Gentile, Mary C. "Keeping Your Colleagues Honest." *Harvard Business Review,* vol. 82, no. 2 (March 2010): 114–117.

Gentile, Mary C., et al. *Giving Voice to Values,* <www.GivingVoiceTo Values.org>.

Gentile, Mary, and Todd D. Jick. "Donna Dubinsky and Apple Computer, Inc. (A)." *Harvard Business School,* 1986. Case no. 395117-PDF-ENG.

Gentile, Mary C., Gary E. Jusela, and William Wiggenhorn. "Raising the Stakes or Finally Seeing Them Clearly? Balanced Leadership in Time of Economic Crisis." *New Academy Review,* vol. 1, no. 1 (February 2002): 37–47.

George, Bill, and Peter Sims. *True North: Discover Your Authentic Leadership.* New York: Jossey-Bass, 2007.

Giacalone, Robert A., Carole L. Jurkiewicz, and Craig Dunn. *Positive Psychology in Business Ethics and Corporate Responsibility.* Greenwich, Conn.: Information Age, 2005.

Gilovich, Thomas. *How We Know What Isn't So: The Fallibility of Human Reason in Everyday Life.* New York: Free Press, 1991.

Gioia, Dennis A. "Pinto Fires and Personal Ethics: A Script Analysis of Missed Opportunities." *Journal of Business Ethics,* vol. 11 (1992): 379–389.

Gladwell, Malcolm. "Here's Why." *New Yorker,* 10 April 2006, <www.new yorker.com/printables/critics/060410crbo_books> (1 September 2009).

Gneezy, Uri. "Deception: The Role of Consequences." *The American Economic Review,* vol. 95, no. 1 (March 2005): 384–394.

Godin, Seth. *All Marketers Are Liars: The Power of Telling Authentic Stories in a Low-Trust World.* New York: Portfolio, 2005.

Greenberg, Jerald, and Marissa S. Edwards, eds. *Voices and Silence in Organizations.* Bingley, U.K.: Emerald Group, 2009.

Haidt, Jonathan. "The Emotional Dog and Its Rational Tail: A Social Intuitionist Approach to Moral Judgment." *Psychological Review,* vol. 108, no. 4 (2001): 814–834.

Haidt, Jonathan. *The Happiness Hypothesis: Finding Modern Truth in Ancient Wisdom.* New York: Basic, 2006.

Handy, Charles. "What's a Business For?" *Harvard Business Review* (December 2002): 49–55.

Hill, Linda, and Suzy Wetlaufer. "Leadership When There Is No One to Ask: An Interview with Eni's Franco Bernabe." *Harvard Business Review* (July-August 1998): 81–94.

Hirschman, Albert O. *Exit, Voice, and Loyalty: Responses to Decline in Firms, Organizations, and States.* Cambridge: Harvard University Press, 1970.

Huneke, Douglas H. *The Moses of Rovno.* New York: Dodd, Mead, 1985.

Ibarra, Herminia. "Provisional Selves: Experimenting with Image and Identity in Professional Adaptation." *Administrative Science Quarterly,* vol. 44, no. 4 (December 1999): 764–791.

Ibarra, Herminia. "What's Your Story?" *Harvard Business Review,* vol. 83, no. 1 (January 2005): 64–71.

Jackall, Robert. *Moral Mazes: The World of Corporate Managers.* New York: Oxford University Press, 1988.

Jackson, Ira A., and Jane Nelson. *Profits with Principles: Seven Strategies for Delivering Value with Values.* New York: Currency Doubleday, 2004.

Janis, Irving L. "Groupthink." *Psychology Today,* vol. 5, no. 6 (November 1971): 43–76.

Johnson, Robert Ann. *Whistle-Blowing: When It Works—And Why.* Boulder, Colo.: Lynne Rienner, 2003.

Kahneman, Daniel, and Amos Tversky, eds. *Choices, Values, and Frames.* New York: Russell Sage Foundation and Cambridge University Press, 2003.

Kane, Robert. *Through the Moral Maze: Searching for Absolute Values in a Pluralistic World.* Armonk, N.Y.: M.E. Sharpe, 1996.

Kegan, Robert, and Lisa Laskow Lahey. "The Real Reason People Won't Change." *Harvard Business Review* (November 2001): 85–92.

Khurana, Rakesh. *From Higher Aims to Hired Hands: The Social Transformation of American Business Schools and the Unfulfilled Promise of Management as a Profession.* Princeton: Princeton University Press, 2007.

Kidder, Rushworth. *How Good People Make Tough Choices: Resolving the Dilemmas of Ethical Living.* New York: HarperCollins, 1995.

Kidder, Rushworth M. *Moral Courage: Taking Action When Your Values Are Put to the Test.* New York: William Morrow, 2005.

Klein, Gary. *Sources of Power: How People Make Decision.* Cambridge: MIT Press, 1998.

Kleiner, Art. *Who Really Matters: The Core Group Theory of Power, Privilege, and Success.* New York: Currency Doubleday, 2005.

Kohut, Heinz. *Self Psychology and the Humanities: Reflections on a New Psychoanalytic Approach.* New York: W.W. Norton, 1985.

Kram, Kathy. *Mentoring at Work.* Lanham, Md.: University Press of America, 1988.

Kram, Kathy, and Belle Rose Ragins. *Handbook of Mentoring at Work: Theory, Research, and Practice.* Thousand Oaks, Calif.: Sage, 2007.

Kristoff, Nicholas D. "When Our Brains Short-Circuit." *New York Times,* 1 July 2009.

Lakoff, George. *Moral Politics: How Liberals and Conservatives Think.* Chicago: University of Chicago Press, 2002.

Landro, Laura. "Bring Surgeons Down to Earth: New Programs Aim to Curb Fear That Prevents Nurses from Flagging Problems." *Wall Street Journal,* 16 November 2005.

Lennick, Doug, and Fred Kiel. *Moral Intelligence: Enhancing Business Performance and Leadership Success.* Upper Saddle River, N.J.: Wharton School Publishing, 2005.

Lewis, Michael. *Liar's Poker: Rising Through the Wreckage on Wall Street.* New York: W.W. Norton, 1989.

Loehr, Jim, and Tony Schwartz. *The Power of Full Engagement: Managing Energy, Not Time, Is the Key to High Performance and Personal Renewal.* New York: Free Press Paperbacks, 2003.

London, Perry. "The Rescuers: Motivational Hypotheses About Christians Who Saved Jews from the Nazis." In *Altruism and Helping Behavior: Social Psychological Studies of Some Antecedents and Consequences,* ed. Jacqueline R. Macaulay and Leonard Berkowitz, pp. 241–250. New York: Academic, 1970.

Lorsch, Jay W., Leslie Berlowitz, and Andy Zelleke, eds. *Restoring Trust in American Business.* Cambridge, Mass.: American Academy of Arts and Sciences, MIT Press, 2005.

MacAvoy, Paul W., and Ira M. Millstein. *The Recurrent Crisis in Corporate Governance.* Stanford, Calif.: Stanford Business, 2004.

Mahan, Brian J. *Forgetting Ourselves on Purpose: Vocation and the Ethics of Ambition.* New York: Jossey-Bass, 2002.

Makar, Stephen D., and Michael A. Pearson. "Earnings Management:

When Does Juggling the Numbers Become Fraud?" *Association of Certified Fraud Examiners,* January-February 2000, <www.acfe.com/fraud/view/asp?ArticleID=124>.

Martin, Roger. "The Wrong Incentive," Editorial Commentary. *Barron's,* vol. 85 (December 2003). <http://online.barrons.com/article/SB10718 7920976382100.html> (2 September 2009).

Martin, Roger. "How Successful Leaders Think." *Harvard Business Review* (June 2007): 60–67.

Messick, David M., and Max H. Bazerman. "Ethical Leadership and the Psychology of Decision-Making." *Sloan Management Review,* vol. 37, no. 2 (Winter 1996): 9–22.

Meyerson, Debra E. *Tempered Radicals: How Everyday Leaders Inspire Change at Work.* Boston: Harvard Business School Press, 2003.

Miller, Danny, and Isabelle Le Breton-Miller. *Managing for the Long Run: Lessons in Competitive Advantage from Great Family Businesses.* Boston: Harvard Business School Press, 2005.

Millstein, Ira. "When Earnings Management Becomes Cooking the Books." *Financial Times Series: Mastering Corporate Governance,* 26 May 2005, 61–68.

Mintzberg, Henry, and Frances Westley. "Decision Making: It's Not What You Think." *MIT Sloan Management Review,* vol. 42, no. 3 (Spring 2001): 89–93.

Mizik, Natalie, and Robert Jacobson. "Myopic Marketing Management: The Phenomenon and Its Long-term Impact on Firm Value." *Marketing Science Institute Working Paper Series,* issue 1, no. 06–001 (2006): 3–21.

Molinsky, Andrew, and Joshua Margolis. "Necessary Evils and Interpersonal Sensitivity in Organizations." *Academy of Management Review,* vol. 30 (2005): 245–268.

Morgan, Gareth. *Images of Organization.* London: Sage, 1986.

Morgan, Gareth. *Imagination: The Art of Creative Management.* London: Sage, 1993.

Morrison, Elizabeth, and Frances J. Milliken. "Organizational Silence: A Barrier to Change and Development in a Pluralistic World." *Academy of Management Review,* vol. 25, no. 4 (2000): 706–725.

O'Toole, James. *The Executive's Compass: Business and the Good Society.* New York: Oxford University Press, 1993.

Paine, Lynn Sharp. *Value Shift: Why Companies Must Merge Social and Financial Imperatives to Achieve Superior Performance.* New York: McGraw-Hill, 2003.

Patterson, Kerry, Joseph Grenny, Ron McMillan, and Al Switzler. *Crucial Conversations: Tools for Talking When Stakes Are High.* New York: McGraw-Hill, 2002.

Pfeffer, Jeffrey, and Robert I. Sutton. *The Knowing-Doing Gap: How Smart Companies Turn Knowledge into Action.* Boston: Harvard Business School Press, 2000.

Plous, Scott. *The Psychology of Judgment and Decision-Making.* New York: McGraw-Hill, 1993.

Pounds, William F. "Why Do Good?" *MIT Sloan Management Review* (Spring 2006): 14–16.

Prentice, Robert. "Teaching Ethics, Heuristics, and Biases." *Journal of Business Ethics Education,* vol. 1, no. 1 (2004): 57–74.

Rapoport, Nancy B., and Bala G. Dharan. *Enron: Corporate Fiascos and Their Implications.* New York: Foundation, 2004.

Ready, Douglas A. "How Storytelling Builds Next-Generation Leaders." *MIT Sloan Management Review,* vol. 43, no. 4 (Summer 2002): 63–69.

Rhode, Deborah L., ed. *Moral Leadership: The Theory and Practice of Power, Judgment, and Policy.* San Francisco: Jossey-Bass, 2006.

Russo, J. Edward, and Paul J. H. Shoemaker. "Managing Overconfidence." *MIT Sloan Management Review,* vol. 33, no. 2 (Winter 1992): 7–17.

Samuelson, Judith, and Mary Gentile. "Get Aggressive About Passivity." *Harvard Business Review* (November 2005): 18–20.

Seligman, Martin E. P. *Authentic Happiness: Using the New Positive Psychology to Realize Your Potential for Lasting Fulfillment.* New York: Simon and Schuster, 2002.

Shanley, John Patrick. *Doubt: A Parable.* New York: Theatre Communications Group, 2005.

Simon, John G., Charles W. Powers, and Jon P. Gunnemann. *The Ethical Investor: Universities and Corporate Responsibility.* New Haven: Yale University Press, 1972.

Simons, Robert. "Control in an Age of Empowerment." *Harvard Business Review* (March-April 1995): 80–88.

Smircich, Linda, and Gareth Morgan. "Leadership: The Management of

Meaning." *The Journal of Applied Behavioral Science,* vol. 18, no. 3 (1 September 1982): 257–273.

Smith, Douglas K. *On Value and Values: Thinking Differently About We . . . in an Age of Me.* Upper Saddle River, N.J.: Financial Times Prentice Hall, 2004.

Smith, H. Jeff. "The Shareholders vs. Stakeholders Debate." *MIT Sloan Management Review,* vol. 44, no. 4 (Summer 2003): 85–90.

Stone, Douglas, Bruce Patton, and Sheila Heen. *Difficult Conversations: How to Discuss What Matters Most.* New York: Penguin, 2000.

Stout, Lynn A. "Bad and Not-So-Bad Arguments for Shareholder Primacy." *UCLA School of Law Research Paper* no. 25, *Law and Economics Research Paper No. 02–04* (2004): 1189–1209.

Tenbrunsel, Anne, and David Messick. "Ethical Fading: The Role of Self-Deception in Unethical Behavior." *Social Justice Research,* vol. 17, no. 2 (June 2004): 223–236.

Thomas, David, John J. Gabarro, and Don Tapscott. *Breaking Through: The Making of Minority Executives in Corporate America.* Boston: Harvard Business School Press, 1999.

Thomas, Terry, John R. Schermerhorn, Jr., and John W. Dienhart. "Strategic Leadership of Ethical Behavior in Business." *Academy of Management Executive,* vol. 18, no. 2 (2004): 56–66.

Turner, Marlene E., ed. *Groups at Work: Theory and Research.* Mahwah, N.J.: Lawrence Erlbaum Associates, 2001.

Vogel, David. *The Market for Virtue: The Potential and Limits of Corporate Social Responsibility.* Washington, D.C.: Brookings Institution Press, 2005.

Webb, Allen P., and Joseph L. Badaracco, Jr. "Business Ethics: A View from the Trenches." *California Management Review,* vol. 37, no. 2 (Winter 1995): 8–28.

Weick, Karl E. "Small Wins: Redefining the Scale of Social Problems." *American Psychologist* (January 1984): 40–49.

Weiser, John, and Simon Zadek. *Conversations with Disbelievers: Persuading Companies to Address Social Challenges.* New York: Ford Foundation, 2000.

"Where Will They Lead: MBA Student Attitudes About Business and Society." A study conducted by the Aspen Institute's Center for Busi-

ness Education, part of the Business and Society Program, <www
.aspencbe.org> (25 January 2009).

Zimbardo, Philip. *The Lucifer Effect: Understanding How Good People
Turn Evil.* New York: Random House, 2008.

# Index